SBP

1
SOCCER TRAINING

Advanced drills for techniques, game strategies, and physical preparation

Written by **Hans Studener**
Werner Wolf

Edited by **Peter Klavora, PhD**
School of Physical
and Health Education
University of Toronto

Sport Books Publisher Toronto

Translation by Linda Paul

Canadian Cataloguing in Publication Data

Studener, Hans
  Soccer training

1st Canadian ed.
Translation of: Fussballtraining.
ISBN 0-920905-26-9 (v. 1)
ISBN 0-920905-28-5 (v. 2)

1. Soccer - Training. I. Wolf, Werner.
II. Klavora, Peter. III. Title.

GV943.9.T7S8313   1990   796.334   C89-094507-1

Distribution in Canada and worldwide by
Sport Books Publisher
278 Robert Street
Toronto, Ontario M5S 2K8

Printed in the United States

Contents

Preface

It seems almost unnecessary to wish this book success. The success it has already achieved has been further extended by subsequent editions of the German original following so quickly. This book will help many coaches and trainers in their daily work. What is especially valuable is that the methods explained here have been proven in practice and will further influence practice. It will bring excitement into the players' creative work and in this way help lead our soccer players to maturity more quickly.

The coaches and instructor are given useful training tips and are provided with an extensive pool of drills and exercises that will strengthen individual training as a major factor in the whole training process. The many simple diagrams are very effective.

The publication of this first English edition is welcomed because of its usefulness in the development of our athletes. We wish success to all the coaches and instructors in the further development of young soccer players capable of increasing the standing of soccer through excellent performance.

Editor

Foreword

This book is based on our successful work with a representative cross section of soccer teams in the German Democratic Republic, including the Olympic team. We have paid special attention to the work of our best coaches in the top league teams, as well as to the experiences that we have gained in practical training at the German Institute of Physical Education (Deutsche Hochschule für Körper Kultur). Both volumes are mainly written for enhancing the versatility of training practice, but they also deal with certain very specific and fundamental factors in training practice, such as, the setup of training sessions and how they should be carried out in the competitive season. To vary training, a large number of drills and exercises are presented that are suitable for the top class level, as well as for young ambitious soccer players.

Our observations are based on game concepts that were predominant at the time this book was published. The game has, of course, changed. Certain aspects of modern soccer are not addressed. In its fundamentals, however, the book remains essentially correct and relevant. It will provide coaches ners and players valuable advice for practical soccer training.

Authors

The Meaning of Modern, Effective Soccer Training?

The demands of soccer have grown. Ever higher performance levels necessary demand a corresponding high level of training. Training combines theoretical and practical knowledge with the physical capabilities of a player during the severe demands of competition. Both require strongly developed physical and psychological capabilities.

A correctly organized training programme will be a motivating force for the constant improvement of performance in soccer. Not only must the level of training be equal to the present performance level of the top world class, it must take into account the *most probable direction* of the game's development. Naturally the experts do not always agree about what this direction will be. The matter is complicated since fundamental ideas about modern soccer, as well as tendencies for its further development, depend upon the approach to training. Bearing these facts in mind we shall begin by discussing our general approach to the modern game and what we believe to be the probable direction of its future development.

Modern Soccer and Its Future Developments

Technique, tempo, toughness—that is modern soccer today. The object of the game a few years ago—to play an interesting game for the spectators—is hardly noticable today. Everything is done for success. In this way, the once much-praised game idea of "block—look—pass" has long since become obsolete. The almost unbeatably good condition of all players at the highest performance levels today, combined with the enjoyment of extremely sophisticated tactics, has led to the disappearance of these outdated approaches to playing the game.

If a team wants to be successful today, speed is of the essence. It must have players in its line-up who know how to combine their technique with fast movement and running speed. The slow players will be replaced by players who can move and run fast as well as master the technical skills. Speed has become an increasingly important factor in soccer performance.

If we look at the development of the soccer game from the tactical side, it becomes more and more evident that the successful teams usually attack from a strong defense. The Brazilian 1:4:2:4 system laid the foundation for this in Sweden in 1958. Since then many variations, such as 1:3:3:4 or 1:3:2:2:3, have appeared. The purpose of all of these tactical systems is to make the opposing forwards' attack on the goal as difficult as possible. Surprise attacks in a wide variety of forms have begun as a result of this counterposition.

At first it seems that the defense has the advantage in the perpetual fight between attack and defense. Indeed, the defense would dominate through a tight defense were the attackers of the opposing team not capable of penetrating with suitable means. These include feinting, dribbling and covered passing, together with polished technique. All of the attacking players—who in our opinion include players in the first, second, and even to some extent the third line—must build their individual skills to the maximum degree, especially in these three elements. A scoring situation can be created against a massive defense only by rational, fast, and exact ball playing. A player gets himself or a teammate into a scoring position only by safely dribbling around two or three opposing players. An accurate covered pass makes the completion of a combination in a small space possible. The team that builds its attack from a specific counterposition also needs players who can perform a difficult game function. But only players who have above average individual skills, especially in feinting, dribbling and covered passing, are able to perform such functions. Internationally successful teams, no matter which systems and tactical variants they use, depend on the abilities of their attackers to exploit scoring opportunities.

All players in the defense; all players in the attack—that is tempo-playing at its fastest. The players' speed, their endurance, their entire mobility, their ability to play without tiring and to maintain a fast game tempo: all of these are used to good effect in this game tactic. Speed guarantees a majority for the attackers for a short time and, on the other hand, can also ensure a majority in the team's own defense against the opposing attackers. Fast action on the soccer field is an important prerequisite of this. A player must pass the ball as soon as possible to be able to move more freely and quickly. Direct passing is demanded. The fast game tempo forces the players to acquire those technical skills that guarantee them speed and safety.

Speed, accuracy, and a fast game tempo are, in themselves, no guarantee of success. Teams and players must also know how to control speed and tempo. They must use tempo and rhythm changes at the right moment to create surprise. Because of this, star players are in more demand than ever. All top European and world teams have the player who has demonstrated an excellent technique and, because of this, can change the tempo and the character of the game easily. He can save strength and release strength at a given moment, vary the tactics, improvise, and finally, make the decisive play. The player who can properly change the tempo of individual moves and the rhythm of the game has at that moment made a considerable step forward and is headed for success. This applies to teams as well as to individual players.

Important Factors in Modern Training

The general approach outlined in the previous sections poses a number of challenges in training. Six in particular should be mentioned.

1. The physical abilities of the player must be applied specifically to soccer and fulfill the demands made on team positions. Physical training should be carried out in combination with the ball and should be set up individually. The fullback must practise more game movements, such as those used in Volume 2, Exercise 62. These exercises are designed to meet the demands made on the fullback in the modern game and to make new and greater physical demands from him. Endurance must receive special attention, corresponding to the radius of the advance of the attack.

2. The technical skills must be simple, fast and effective. What once were very important technical skills have become almost superfluous, i.e., blocking, which is being replaced more and more by moving the ball forward, because of today's more efficient game. Some technical skills such as the feint, dribbling, and the covered pass have gained in importance and have been perfected.

3. The excellent condition of all players in the last few years has led more and more to man-to-man fighting. In addition to more intensive one-on-one training, however, new, more effective methods should be found to make it possible to lose the opponent. For example, getting into the open to recieve a pass from a teammate requires timing. And controlling the ball without interception can only be achieved in conjunction with sprinting.

4. All scoring opportunities should be exploited. Goal shots should be forced more than ever and set up in various simulated game situations. The defender should also be included in the goal-shot training. Carry out the goal shot practice as if it were a real game.

5. Change of tempo and rhythm should be taught in all technical and tactical game actions. The player must be able to exploit tempo change in all game situations.

6. Certain technical and tactical game manoeuvres must be established in such a way that the speed, precision and tempo of the game action can be further increased. We have listed some game moves that can become so automatic that room for creative playing is increased and is encouraged as much as possible.

Passing, Sprinting and Getting into the Open

It is important that the sprint has already begun at the moment of the pass. This increases the speed of the game. The opponent can be outplayed without dribbling, therefore largely avoiding the risk of losing the ball while dribbling. The bad habit of dribbling the ball for a long time will be surpressed and the midfield will be crossed more quickly.

The Wall Pass (see Exercise 162)

Four important points should be noted:
1. make a strong covered pass to your teammate;
2. pass accurately to avoid difficulties for your teammate;
3. begin sprinting during the pass;

4. pass the ball.

By mastering the wall pass, an attack can succeed even in limited space. The opponent will eventually become unsure and will hesitate in his defense. At precisely that moment, the team should attack.

Getting into the Open—Sprinting and Timing

Getting into the open requires timing. The following basic rule holds true: before a player receives the ball, he must look for an immediate opportunity to pass. If the ball has already been received, the player looks for an opportunity to pass only after he has the ball under control. In both cases, the recognition must be immediate and automatic.

Running toward or away (getting into the open) may only take place by sprinting with precise timing. In the man-to-man marking generally practised today, getting possession of the ball or shooting for the goal unhindered is possible only within very precise margins. A good starting position is needed to be able to get into the open. Those players who are not playing defense must watch for the right time, even when the opponent has the ball. The players of the first attacking line must lure their opposing players away from the opposing goal. If they succeed in doing this effectively, a large avenue of attack will have been created, an avenue through which it should become possible to sprint back to forward positions.

The Covered Pass

The ball should, if possible, be passed with the outer instep. The kicking movement must be short, coming mainly from the ankle. The direction of the pass should not be betrayed by any movement before the kick. Take a different passing direction through effective feinting. The covered pass gains increasing importance as the free space in front of the goal becomes smaller. Endurance is generally increased through intensive training. Tactical variations providing for the attack from a strengthened defense also leaves little space in front of the goal for counterattack. Under these circumstances, the completion of a combination is only possible through exact, accurate and covered passes.

Immediate Interception After Loss of Ball:
Acquiring Confidence to Dribble in the Attack Zone

Breaking through a mass defense and creating a scoring possibility for oneself or a teammate, is often only possible through dribbling. Dribbling, however, can only be effective if it is mastered. It must be learned properly and, above all, continually practised in the game.

Every player knows that the danger of losing the ball while dribbling is very great. Because of this, some players are afraid to dribble. Dribbling takes place mainly in midfield where it is more successful. It is rarely used in front of the opposing goal because limited space and the strong defense of opposing players make successful dribbling difficult. If unsuccessful dribbling is met with reproaches by teammates, it is certain that it will not be tried again. "If a technique is not constantly practised, it will not be mastered; if it is not mastered, it will not be willingly done, or done only hesitantly." This basic statement, which is applicable to all sports, has special significance for dribbling in soccer. Again, dribbling must be constantly practised. Fear of losing the ball must be eliminated. The first step is training the players to intercept immediately after the ball Is lost. With appropriate training, the ball is often quickly recaptured; or one's own team gets the ball back quickly by forcing opposing players to make uncontrolled passes. This builds self-confidence. The opponent becomes nervous, and other game advantages can arise.

Dribbling at Varied Tempo

Fast playing alone does not guarantee success if the opponent is also fast and can counter with appropriate tactics. The same applies to the movements of individual players. For this reason, fast dribbling alone does not create decisive advantages. The defenders will adapt quickly to the tempo. Only players who know how to change the tempo while dribbling have an advantage in the modern game. What is important is that the change in tempo surprises the opposing player.

You should familiarize yourselves with the six technical and tactical game moves described in the previous pages. Practise a few simple general motor skills. Let us note, however, that the modern game, because of the tremendous development of soccer, requires more technical and tactical game manoeuvres. Making these automatic is not easy in soccer. Not all movement skills become second nature through training alone, such that they can be translated into action during competition. They must be further developed under competitive conditions so that the skills become relatively stable and cannot be disrupted through outside stimuli. In soccer there are great differences between practice and competition environments. Because of this the danger arises that these specific movement skills will not be carried out, or will be performed only with some hesitation because of the great risk. To make the moves automatic, it is recommended that a further step be introduced into the process: the use of practice games and drills, set up along the lines outlined below in *Suggestions for the Effective Structure of a Training Unit.*

Training Tasks and Goals in the Competitive Season

New movements in sport are created under specific conditions. In soccer, the conditions must also be appropriate to the modern game, which makes higher demands on technique, tactics, and the physical shape of the players. All these factors must be complementary. Because the game makes higher demands on the players than training does, practice must be designed correspondingly. These can be created by more extensive training, and by new and better training methods, which place higher demands on players.

The stress of competition for soccer players is spread over the entire year. Because of this, the problem of training year-round in soccer, in comparison to other sports, was solved much earlier and the solution has long since become natural. Lately, however, the training year has been systematically divided into seasons. This has been done in many countries for several years. The training year is divided into the preparation, the peak and the transitory season. Each of the seasons has specific goals and tasks. The higher the expectations the more thorough the training in these periods must be. The stress level and contents must correspond to the training condition and to the tasks that must be solved. The training must be carried out in such a way that the player goes to competition-sphysically and psychologically prepared.

Thus it makes a difference how a player trains during the year. First a good general preparation for the competitive season is necessary. Then the players and team must be brought into competitive readiness. Once this stage has been reached, it must be maintained. All-round, tough training is a good foundation.

The competitive readiness must however be improved at specific times. If certain very strong opponents or teams are to be effectively challenged, the team must be in the very best condition at that specific time. Such top form is usually necessary several times during the competitive season.

In addition to this the team's game must be constantly improved and further developed in the light of the latest advancements. The capabilities and skills of the players must be constantly improved and expanded.

The three main tasks to be emphasized are:

- maintaining a good competitive form over the entire championship season;
- achieving top performance for very specific competitions;
- constantly improving the playing level of the team and players during training in the peak competitive season.

League games inevitably make the greatest demands on top class players. Strength and nerves will be required, most of all, from them. Their competition season extends the longest because of many international obligations, so training in the main season must be set up in such a way that their strength and emotional energy can be renewed. Every coach knows how difficult this can be in practice. Finding the right level of stress, as well as the appropriate exercises, takes a lot of experience.

For players frequently exposed to psychological stress, soccer games in training during these periods should be kept to a minimum, especially practice with teammates, such as team games and games with two goals. On the other hand, exercises like the many presented in this book should be stressed.

Frequent training in the week is necessary for a top class player. Such training should make him technically and tactically capable of carrying out everything required in competition. Since the demands of modern soccer have increased, the players already regard frequent training as a necessity. A great danger in frequent training, however, is monotony. Monotony leads to loss of interest and desire to cut short training sessions. Training must have an emotional foundation, even when it is carried out purposefully and seriously and hard demands are made. It must be all-around and varied in nature. It must produce demonstrable improvement in performance, and it must be enjoyable.

Young soccer players are drawn to soccer, despite obligations, because it fulfils their need for movement and competition. Their playing instinct is satisfied by soccer. They want to be good soccer players and emulate their idols. This assumption plays an extremely important role in setting up training. The goal of training for players in the youth category—juniors, youths, pupils and children—must use the emotional factors.

Running practice in combination with the ball is always fun for young soccer players. For them, no way is too long, no exertion too hard. These drills will bring alive their playing instinct. To satisfy their competetive spirit, conditions must be created in which competetive elements predominate. Above all, games must include goal shots. In contrast to the recommendations for top class players, games should be part of training even during the peak season. They can be played without limitation in all variations. Training with the ball that takes into account the fun of playing; and competitive spirit creates the right atmosphere for young soccer players.

The development of young soccer players should not be one-sided. The principle of all-round training must predominate, by encouraging not only technical and tactical training, but also all-round fitness training. Learning complicated skills can be achieved more quickly within the available training time if driills with the ball are allowed to become the focus. Fitness training should be combined with the technical elements of soccer training. This is a basic requirement not only for training in the main season but also for the preparation season.

The Effective Structure of a Training Unit in the Competitive Season

It has already been stressed that it is very important to make the content of specific training units as much like the content of competitive games as possible. The players should occupy themselves almost exclusively with the ball. All movements without the ball are carried out as in a soccer match, either going away from or toward the ball.

The example of a training unit presented in this section has been especially designed for the technique, tactics, fitness, and stress load of competitive situations. First we will provide a general explanation of the set-up of a training unit, referring particularly to stress and structure.

Structure and Stress Load of a Training Unit

Each training unit has a certain methodological structure. This structure is based on several physiological, and pedagogical-psychological principles. Normally a training unit is divided into three sections: introduction, main part, and conclusion.

Introduction

The introductory part prepares all systems of the organism, as well as awakening the joy in performance and readiness of the player. The physiological processes in the human organism are slowly prepared from normal expectations for the intensive movements and stress of training. The player must be put into the right mood psychologically. The condition of the nervous system must be improved through effective training to increase the readiness necessary for strenuous physical activity and concentrated exercise. The temperature of the muscles is gradually raised by the slowly increasing stress in this preliminary part.

In the introductory part, the coach should take into account the state of training already reached, as well as the expected demands in the main part. The players must be prepared for the stress of the main part by the end of the warm-up. The means used should also refer to the material in this part, because a continuous transition encourages the realization of the purpose of the main part.

Main Part

The coach must have a specific aim for each training unit. This aim determines the character of the training in the main part. To achieve this aim, the coach assigns the player certain tasks dealing with technique, tactics or fitness. They will, however, never appear in a pure form in training with the ball, because most of the drills are complex. Nevertheless, the different elements are given priority in the drill according to the tasks assigned. The choice of material is not, by itself, decisive for the character of the training session. The main points briefly indicated in every drill are also important.

The main part takes up the greatest time in a training unit: 60% to 70% of the entire training time. Normally, players begin with exercises to learn new technical or tactical elements, or with speed exercises. The stress gradually increases. Most attention should be paid to accuracy and good performance. Afterwards the elements already known and practised earlier will be competetively and intensively practised. Fast movements combined with the right tempo changes now have main importance. The highest stress is usually reached in this section.

Conclusion

Following strenuous work performed in the main part of the trainings sessions the athletes should progressively decrease the training effort in order to approach their initial, pre-training biological and psychological states. At the end of the main part of a practice session, most of the athelete's functions are operating at close to maximum capacity and the progressive return to a less demanding activity is necessary. The main motive is not only the fact that an abrupt interruption of effort may have negative physiological and psychological effects on the athlete, but that through warm-down the rate of recovery is significantly enhanced.

The Control of Stress in Training

The amount of stress in training is naturally different throughout the year. While it is gradually increased to the maximum limit in the preparation season, it is generally maintained at a lower level in the peak season. It should be adjusted to the training condition and to the tasks to be solved. The better their condition after preparatory training, the harder the players can train in the peak season. It is certain that tough all-round training during the peak season is a major requirement for good competetive fitness. In contrast to the preparation time, the training stress load must equal that required in competition during the peak season. Not every game has the same physical and psychological effects. If large reserves of strength and psychological energy are demanded, these must be trained for in the next training session. The stress will usually be less. With a less strenuous game, it is the opposite.

Training during the competition season should be geared not merely to the stress of the previous game; it is often more important that forthcoming tasks be taken into consideration. Teams and players must be prepared in such a way that they are sufficiently fit to win the competition. Opponents are not of equal strength. Training stress must take this factor into account as well. Experience has shown that increased stress is not productive until later. In turn, a reduction in training stress can have detrimental effects after a short time, but is followed immediately by a temporary increase in performance. Therefore, training stress should never remain the same throughout the entire competition season. Weeks with heavier stress will inevitably alternate with weeks in which the stress is reduced. Toward the end of the season, in most cases the training stress is successfully reduced gradually over a few weeks. Naturally there is no recipe for this. The experience and skill of the coach are the decisive factors for success.

The training sessions throughout the week also have different amounts of stress, just as the stress differs from week to week. Days of strenuous training are combined with days of medium or minimum stress.

Illustrated Example of a Practice Session During the Competitive Season

I. Introduction

25 min.—agility exercises and tempo runs ; 5 minutes of flexibility work.

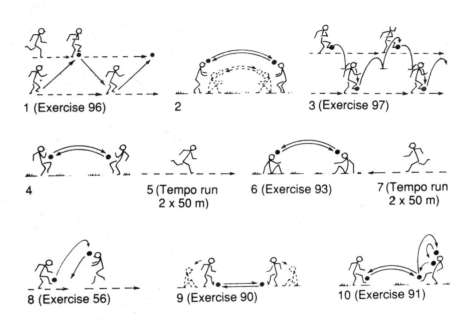

1 (Exercise 96)   2   3 (Exercise 97)

4   5 (Tempo run   6 (Exercise 93)   7 (Tempo run
                    2 x 50 m)   2 x 50 m)

8 (Exercise 56)   9 (Exercise 90)   10 (Exercise 91)

II. Main Part

15 min.—Sprint Toward the Ball

1 (Exercise 166)

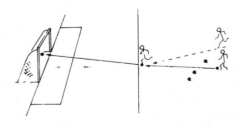

2 (Exercise 167)

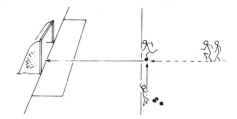

3 (Exercise 165)

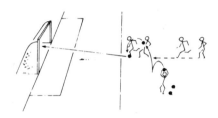

35 min.—Exercises for Forwards

1 (Exercise 109)

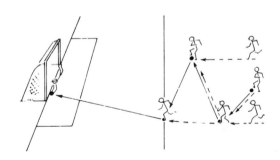

2 (Exercise 156)

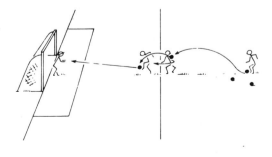

3 (Exercise 111)

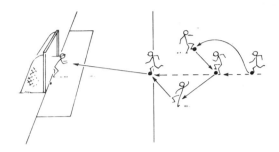

35 min.—Exercises for Defenders

1 (Exercise 99)

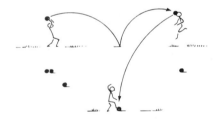

2 (Exercise 45, Volume 2)

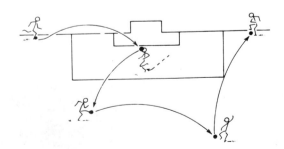

3 (Exercise 44, Volume 2)

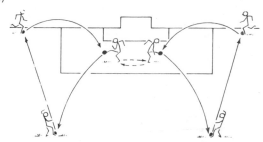

III. Conclusion

10 min.—Final Shots

Suggestions for the Effective Structure of a Training Unit

In illustrations 1 and 2 one can see that we have kept to the general principles of the structure of stress. The intoductory part to soccer training includes specific material, mainly consisting of exercises that develop a feeling for the ball. The exercises alternate rapidly with movements without the ball through which the change in stimulus which the game demands is achieved. Naturally intensity gradually increases as the exercises develop.

This warm-up makes high demands on the concentration of the player. The stress on the organs and muscles alternates constantly with the training of concentration. This effective stress load allows intensive practice. The main part of the training session is primarily filled out with more complex exercise material taken from soccer or from games with similar movement patterns. With these exercises, several elements of the game, such as technique, tactics and conditioning are trained at the same time. Depending on the purpose, however, the coach will give one or the other element priority. The main part of the illustrated sample training unit, according to its organization, comes from position training. The exercises given are complex. It is up to the coach which element should be given priority in training. If improving technique requires special attention, the coach will be concerned less with speed of execution and more with exact technical execution. If tactics of the players are weak, the coach will have to emphasize precision passing, getting in the open in various situations, and to proper kicking method. If conditioning is most important, attention should be given to an intensive exercise completion. Good training organization is a prerequisite for all three main points.

Many balls are necessary for a training programme that makes exercises with the ball its main component. The more balls available, the easier and better the training will be. Plastic balls, which are considerably less expensive than leather, can be used. Getting a large net (10 x 25) to set up behind the goal is much more difficult. We feel confident, however, that many sports organizations would set up such a net if they knew how useful the net is in intensive goal-shot training. The cost is far less than putting up a shooting wall. Other effective and helpful materials are moveable standard goals made of lightweight tubes, wooden rebound walls, flagstaffs, and high jump stands.

Only all-round training can be effective. According to this principle, we offer a variety of exercises with the appropriate description. An improvement in individual performance is primarily achieved with an organized all-year training programme. A good team, however, is not successful through the individual achievements of their players alone. It is also not enough if indidividual parts of the team work well together. The most important factor is an exemplary team harmony. To create this, and also to consolidate the practised game moves, practice games are necessary. The opponent can be a local team. The choice of opponent must be according to the tasks assigned. The practice game should be without spectators to preserve its character.

Often practice games will be played against one's own teammates due to lack of suitable opponents. Such games, however, usually do not fulfil the desired purpose because the players know each other too well. As a result, game situations arise other than those that would arise in competition. Technical and tactical game manoeuvres are therefore not as practised and automatic as required in competition.

These practice games are still better than two goal-games with teammates, games that take place on a reduced playing area and with small field handball goals instead of the normal soccer goals. Soccer players enjoy playing these games; and this tempts coaches and trainers to set them up frequently. The enthusiasm these games create in the players should make greater training stress possible, and they are just right for certain levels of soccer. They are especially recommended for young players. But the constant repetition involved is a serious disadvantage for advanced players. Game manoeuvres that limit successful playing in competition become routine in these practice games.

Top international teams take advantage of goal opportunities. However, many forwards have a tendency to shoot at the goal from close up instead of looking for a goal corner and making a positioned goal shot. It has been further noted that many chances are lost because the player passes once too often instead of shooting on the goal from a distance of 16 to 20 m. If we examine this problem in the light of the two-goal pratice games, it becomes clear that the two-goal practice game is at fault. Goals in such games are usually only scored from a short distance and with a very hard shot. With small goals there is almost no other way to overcome the goalkeeper. Since it is a small-scale game, players often try to make a concerted move up to the goal. An almost exclusive emphasis on short and elaborate passing with many back passes, slow game tempo, and the lack of wing passing are further detrimental effects of theses games.

Therefore practise games should be played whenever possible against unknown competitors under normal competition conditions with the proper uniform. The only legitimate exceptions are that there can be no spectators and that the games are directed by the coach himself, so that he can make more thorough corrections from a better position during the game. Such corrections and comments will be more carefully noted by the players in practice than they would be in formal competition.

The score is not what counts. Certain game moves and tactical manoeuvres usually taught in training take priority. This kind of training offers the soccer player the only chance to train under realistic conditions and to practise specific technical and tactical game moves without risk so that they can be successfully used in official competitions.

General Practice Drills

Symbols used in this book

--→	the player's running path	WF	wing forward
──→	path of the ball	OR	outside right
⤳	dribbling	OL	outside left
GK	goalkeeper	IF	inside forward
FB	fullback	IR	inside right
RB	right back	IL	inside left
LB	left back	CF	centre forward
CB	centre back	FP	field player
HB	halfback	CO	coach
RH	right half	OP	opponent
LH	left half	A. B. C.	players of the
FO	forward	D. E. F	groups A. B. C.
			D. E. F

Ex. 1

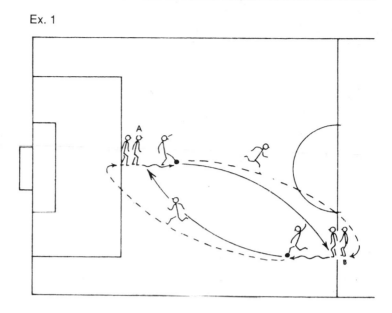

1

Participants   4 - 8 FP

Equipment   1 ball

Description   The players are divided into two groups. They stand about 30 - 40 m apart diagonally across from each other. The first player of group A makes a high centre pass to the first player of group B. He controls the ball, dribbles it a few steps, then passes it half-high mid to upper body height to the second player of group A. This is practised continously. Immediately after kicking, each player sprints to the end of the other group.

Objectives   1. Accurate half high passing.
2. Fast ball control.
3. Passing and sprinting.
4. Building speed endurance.

Comments   If possible, structure the exercise so that the players must also pass diagonally to the playing field. The fewer the players, the more intensive the excercise. With four players, for example, not only is passing made more intensive, endurance is improved.

Ex. 2

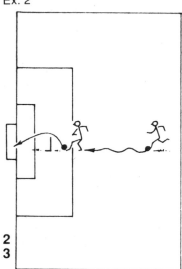

2
3

Ex. 3

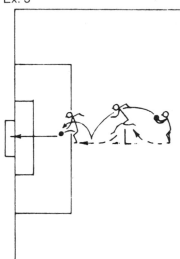

Participants   1 - 8 FP   1 GK

Equipment   1 ball for each player
              1 hurdle

Description   **Exercise 2:** Set up a hurdle about 11 m in front of the goal to represent a goalkeeper lying down. The player runs to the hurdle with the ball on his foot and, while running full speed, lifts the ball over the hurdle into the goal.

              Exercise 3: Set up a hurdle about 25 m in front of the goal, with a player 4 m in front of it. The first player throws the ball in an arc over the hurdle and shoots the ball out of the air into the goal before his second jump.

Objectives   1. Fast proper dribbling (exercise 2).
              2. Lifting the rolling ball while running at full speed (exercise 2).
              3. Improving speed (Exercise 3).
              4. Improving jumping ability and agility.

Comments   All players stand in a line so that the exercise can be played continuously. Exercise 2 is well suited to the intoductory part of a training session. Exercise 3 can be played very well in competition. After each successful kick, the player may take position 1 m further from the hurdle. The player who succeeds in scoring a goal from the greatest distance before touching the ground a second time is the winner.

Ex. 4

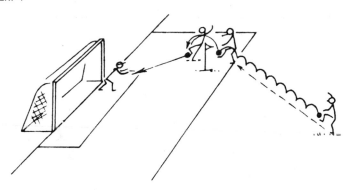

4

Participants 1 - 8 FP   1 GK

Equipment   1 ball for each player
             1 flagstaff

Description A flagstaff is set up in an inside right position in the penalty area.
             From the middle of the goal, about 25 m away, the player juggles
             the ball while walking around the flagstaff and immediately shoots
             for the goal from this cover. The ball may not touch the ground until
             the goal shot.

Objectives   1. Improving feel for the ball.
             2. Goal shot from cover.
             3. Following up the goal shot.

Comments   All players line up so that practice can go on without interruption.
             After the goal shot, each player sprints after his ball and dribbles it
             slowly to the end of the line. This exercise can be used effectively
             in the introductory part of a training session. To increase the
             intensity, have the players juggle while running.

Ex. 5   Ex. 6

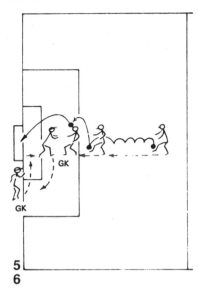

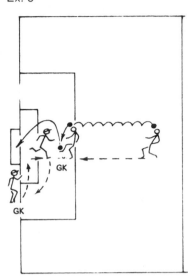

5
6

Participants   1 - 8 FP   2 GK

Equipment   1 ball for each player

Description   **Exercise 5:** The players line up about 25 m in front of the goal. The first player juggles the ball with his foot toward the goal. As soon as he reaches the penalty area, the goalkeeper runs up to the player. The player now plays the ball quickly from his foot to his head and heads it over the goalkeeper into the goal. The second goalkeeper concentrates on this player while the first runs back to the side of the goal.

Exercise 6: as in Exercise 5. Now the player juggles the ball with his head and kicks it with his foot over the goalkeeper into the goal.

Objectives   1. Improving feel for the ball
2. Training indirect vision: have the players watch the goalkeeper when juggling.

Comments   To encourage a fast pace, each player fetches his own ball and runs slowly outside of the playing area to the end of his group. The exercise is well-suited to the introductory part of a training hour. The level of difficulty can be increased if the juggling is done while running.

Ex. 7

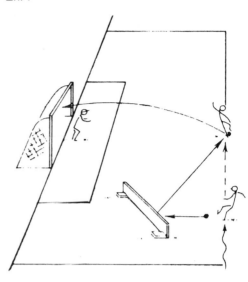

7

Participants   1 - 10 FP   1 GK

Equipment   1 ball for each player
                1 rebound wall (? m long, 1 m high)

Description   The rebound wall is set up in the penalty area as shown in the
                drawing. The players line up. The first player dribbles the ball along
                the penalty area boundary and kicks a strong, low pass against the
                rebound wall. He immediately runs on and shoots the ball, which
                has rebounded, into the goal.

Objectives   1. Strong, low passing (as preparation for the wall pass).
                2. Passing and sprinting.
                3. Goal shot from a slight turn.
                4. Following up the goal shot.

Comments   Each player sprints to fetch the ball shot at the goal and dribbles it
                outside of the shooting area to the starting position at the end of the
                group. The coach can change the angle of the rebound wall after a
                while. This creates a new new situation for the players.

Ex. 8

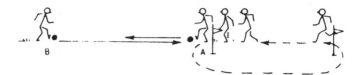

Ex. 9

8
9

Participants   A = 2 - 5 FP   B = 1 GK

Equipment   1 ball
2 flagstaffs

Description   **Exercise 8:** The flagstaffs are set up 10 m apart. The distance between B and the first player of group A is 5 m. Player A makes a low, strong pass to player B and sprints immediately around the flagstaffs to the end of his group. Player B lets the ball rebound gently to the next player in group A.

Exercise 9: Set up as in Exercise 8. Player A makes a low, strong pass to B and immediately sprints around the flagstaffs to position B. Player B lets the ball bounce back and immediately sprints to the end of group A. The second player of group A makes a low, strong pass to position B.

Objectives   1. Strong. low passing to a player.
2. Passing and sprinting.
3. Letting the ball rebound gently.

Comments   In Exercise 8. player B is replaced after a certain time. If there are only few players, this exercise is very useful to teach endurance. If there are many players. form several relay groups which compete in passing.

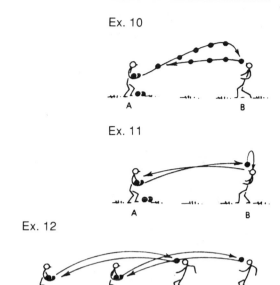

Ex. 10

Ex. 11

Ex. 12

10
11
12

Participants   2 FP = one group
Several groups can practise at the same time

Equipment   2 balls for each group

Description   **Exercise 10:** Player A rapidly throws the balls up, one after the other, to player B, who heads them directly back.

Exercise 11: As in exercise 10. Player B, however, does not head the ball back directly but hits it with his head once first.

Exercise 12: As in exercise 10. Both partners move toward a previously determined point. B runs backwards and heads from a jump.

Objectives   1. Accurate passing with the head.
2. Building concentration.
3. Improving jumping ability (exercise 12).

Comments   Balls used in this exercise should be of the same size and weight. If teaching concentration is the main objective , pay attention to a rapid exercise pace.

Ex. 13

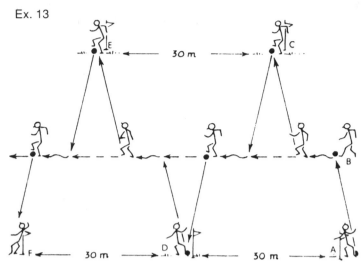

13

Participants   6 - 8 FP

Equipment   1 ball for each player of group A
               5 flagstaffs

Description   The positions of players B to F are marked with flagstaffs. The
               spaces in between are 30 m, the distances 10 m.
               Player A passes diagonally and low to B. Player B dribbles the ball
               and passes it diagonally, low and strong, to C and sprints forward.
               Player C deflects the ball into B's running path. B briefly takes it
               along and makes another diagonal low, strong pass to D, who
               deflects the ball into B's running path. The practice continues in
               this way until the ball reaches player F. After the deflection from F,
               B takes the ball along briefly, plays it back high to the starting
               position, and then goes to position F. All the players posted at the
               flagstaffs change positions against the playing direction; F to E, E
               to D, D to C, C to A, and A has already changed to B. Even before
               the first player of group A has passed the ball back to the starting
               position, the next player of group A has started.

Objectives   1. Teaching the wall pass.
               2. Improvement of endurance.

Comments   To achieve perfect completion of the individual game moves, a
               level playing surface is necessary. If special importance is given to
               the improvement of endurance, the CO should pay attention to in-
               tensive exercise completion. For the technical and tactical game
               moves in the wall pass, see page 10.

Ex. 14

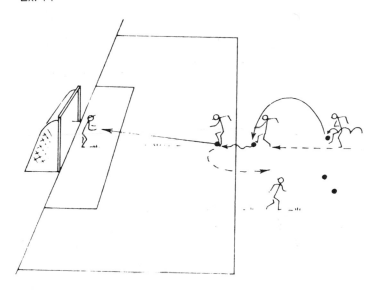

14

Participants   1 - 8 FP   1 GK

Equipment   1 ball for every player

Description   The player juggles the ball with his feet at a slow run up to 25 m in front of the goal. He then kicks the ball into the air in an arc 5 m ahead, runs after it, moves it forward into the penalty area and shoots for the goal.

Objectives   1. Getting used to the ball.
2. Gaining control quickly of a high ball.
3. Making a positioned goal shot.
4. Following up the goal shot.

Comments   Each player fetches the ball he has shot at the goal and goes outside of the shooting zone back to his starting position. If this exercise is used in the introductory part of a training session, the goal shot should be made with minimal exertion.

Ex. 15

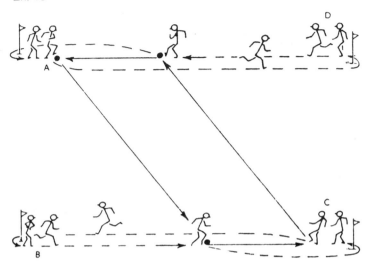

15

Participants   8 - 12 FP

Equipment   1 ball
4 flagstaffs

Description   Set up the flagstaffs in a rectangle, about 30 m long and 10 m wide.
The distances may be varied.
The first player of group B sprints to position C. The first player of
group A immediately makes a strong, low pass into B's running
path. B passes directly to the first player of group C. At the same
moment, the first player of group D sprints to position A, so that C
can pass directly into D's running path. D passes the ball back to A.
Players A and D, as well as B and C, exchange their positions after
passing.

Objectives   1. Strong, low passing into a teammate's running path.
2. Passing and sprinting.
3. Direct, low passing to a player.
4. Getting into the open at the right moment.

Comments   Less experienced players stop the ball first with the inside of the
foot. This must be remembered when getting into the clear.
Experienced players pass the ball directly with the outer instep. Endurance can be developed more effectively if two players are
available in every group and the exercise is done quickly.

Ex. 16

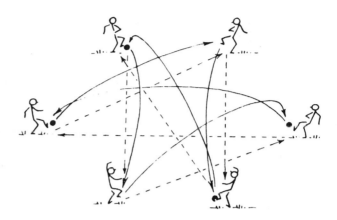

16

Participants   5 - 7 FP

Equipment   1 ball

Description   The players form a circle with a radius of about 25 m. The ball is passed directly half-high. After passing, each player runs to the position he has just passed to.

Objectives   1. Making an accurate half-high pass to a player.
2. Passing and sprinting.

Comments   With less experienced players, the ball is first stopped before being passed to a partner. If this exercise is used in the introductory part of the training session, each player runs to his new position at a moderate speed after passing.
The fewer number of participants, the more intensive the exercise.

Ex. 17

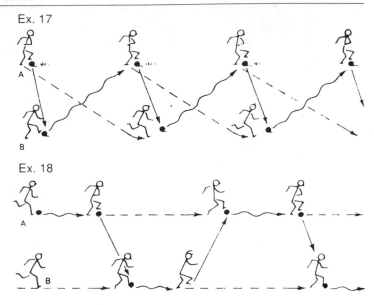

Ex. 18

17
18

Participants   2 FP = one group
Several groups can play in sequence.

Equipment   1 ball for each group

Description   **Exercise 17:** A passes into B's running path. B takes the ball along and crosses over to A's side. Player A has run to the right side after B, and while running receives the pass from B.

Exercise 18: Player A dribbles the ball a few steps. As soon as B starts to sprint, A makes a strong, low pass into B's running path and sprints forward. Player B takes the ball along briefly, then passes it into A's running path and sprints forward.

Objectives   1. Strong, low passing into a teammate's running path.
2. Passing and sprinting.
3. Moving the ball forward quickly.
4. Proper position change (Exercise 17).

Comments   Both exercises can be used comprehensively:
1) in the introductory part of a training session with less intensive exercising;
2) in the main part with very intensive exercising to teach endurance; and
3) in both parts to teach rhythm change.

Ex. 19

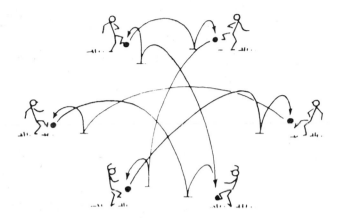

19

Participants 5 - 7 FP

Equipment 1 ball

Description The players form a circle with a radius of about 30 m. The ball is passed high. The pass must be calculated so that it reaches the partner after bouncing only once. The ball must not be passed too forcefully, so that it can be easily passed farther with direct passing.

Objectives 1. Accurate passing to a player.
2. Controlling a bouncing ball.

Comments The circle is made as small as possible for less experienced players. At first they pass the ball with the inside of the foot.
The circle should be as large as possible for experienced players. They pass with the instep or outer instep.

Ex. 20

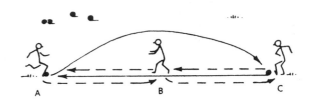

Ex. 21

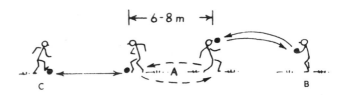

20
21

Participants   3 FP = one group
                Several groups can practise at the same time.

Equipment   1 ball for exercise 20
                1 ball for exercise 21

Description   **Exercise 20:** Three players stand in a line at a distance of 5 m.
                Players B and C face A. Player A passes the ball over B to C and
                immediately changes positions with B. Player C receives the ball
                and passes it between the straddled legs of Player A. now standing
                in the middle. to B and changes positions with A. Now B passes over
                C to player A and the positions are changed again in the same way.

                Exercise 21: Player B throws the ball high to A who immediately
                heads it back and quickly turns around. C passes a low ball to him
                right away. which he deflects gently. He turns around quickly again
                and B throws him another high ball.

Objectives   1. Accurate passing to a player.
                2. Passing and sprinting.
                3. Accurate heading back.
                4. Letting the ball rebound gently.

Comments   These exercises are well suited to less experienced players. For
                advanced players they are used in the introductory part. With
                intensive exercising. they teach concentration very effectively.

Ex. 22

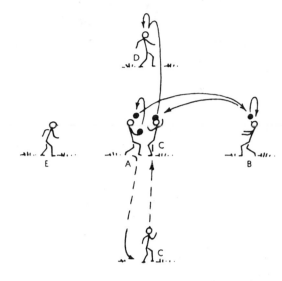

22

Participants   5 FP

Equipment   1 ball

Description   The players stand as shown in the diagram. The distance to A is 3 m. A heads the ball to B and runs to C, who immediately leaves his position and runs to the middle. Meanwhile B has headed the ball up once and then to the middle. Player C heads the ball directly to D and runs to B, who has immediately left his position and run to the middle. He heads the ball headed back by D to E. The ball goes around in this strict order and the position changes always take place so that a player changes with the player on his right after the pass.

Objectives   1. Accurate heading.
2. Controlling the ball with the head.
3. Heading and running.

Comments   Five players are necessary for this game or the planned order cannot be kept. The distance to player A is increased with advanced players.

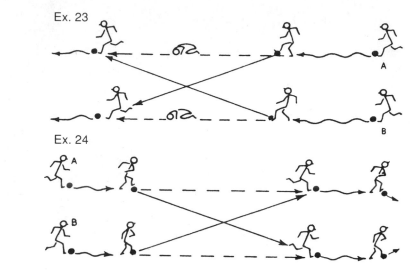

Ex. 23

Ex. 24

23
24

Participants 2 FP = one group
Several groups can play in sequence.

Equipment 1 ball for each player

Description **Exercise 23:** Players A and B are 5 m apart. Both players move towards a specified target. Each player dribbles the ball a few steps. At a signal from A, they pass their balls diagonally into their partner's running path, do a quick forward roll, and sprint after their partner's ball, taking it along and dribbling it a few steps. On A's command, the passing begins again.

Exercise 24: As in Exercise 23, but without the forward roll.

Objectives 1. Correct slow dribbling.
2. Accurate passing into the partner's running path.
3. Moving the ball forward quickly.
4. Correct rhythm change.
5. Improving agility.

Comments These exercises can be used in many ways:
1. in the introductory part of the training session with less intensive exercising;
2. in the main part with very intensive exercising to teach endurance; and
3. to teach rhythm change. After dribbling slowly, pass and sprint to partner's ball.

Ex. 25

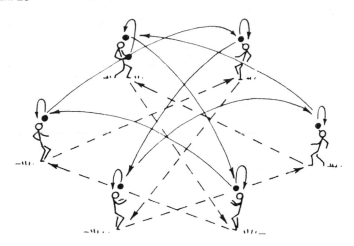

25

Participants 4 - 7 FP

Equipment 1 ball

Description The players form a circle with a radius of about 8 m. The ball is headed to any player. Each player heads the ball up before passing it on. Players run immediately to the position to which they headed.

Objectives 1. Accurate heading.
2. Controlling the ball with the head.
3. Heading and running.

Comments This is a very good exercise for the introductory part of a training session. If there are more than seven players, they are divided into two groups. Endurance can be taught in the main part of the training session. For this exercise the radius of the circle is increased and the players sprint to the new position after the pass.

Ex. 26

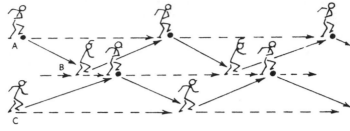

Ex. 27

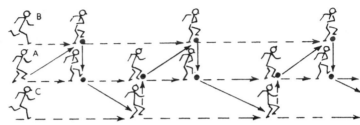

26
27

Participants 3 FP = one group
Several groups can play in sequence.

Equipment 2 balls for each group (Exercise 26)
1 ball for each group (Exercise 27)

Description **Exercise 26:** Three players stand at the same level 5 m apart. Player B sprints forward and receives a pass in his running path from A. B deflects the ball into A's running path and quickly turns around. Now player C passes a ball into B's running path which he deflects into C's running path. He immediately sprints forward to call for the next path from A. Players A and C dribble the ball until B calls for a pass.

Exercise 27: Player A passes the ball diagonally into B's running path. Then B deflects the ball at a right angle to his running direction into A's running path. Player A now passes diagonally into C's running path. C deflects the ball at a right angle to his own running direction into A's running path.

Objectives 1. Accurate. low passing into a teammate's running path.
2. Letting the ball rebound gently.
3. Passing and sprinting.

Comments These exercises. known as combination forms. can be used in many ways: 1. in the introductory part of a training session with less intensive exercising: 2. in the main part with very intensive exercising to teach endurance: 3. in both parts to teach rhythm change.

Ex. 28

28

Participants 5 - 10 FP

Equipment 1 ball

Description A circle is formed. The central circle in midfield is suitable for quick orientation. In the middle of the circle is a player with the ball. He heads the ball to one partner and immediately sprints to another, who immediately leaves his position and sprints to the middle of the circle. The player to whom the ball has been passed heads the ball back to the middle of the circle. The player who has sprinted to the middle catches the ball and begins again.

Objectives 1. Accurate heading.
2. Passing and sprinting.
3. Immediately leaving a new position when a partner runs to it.

Comments With experienced players, the player who has just run back into the circle does not catch the ball, but heads it directly to one point and sprints immediately to another. The exercise is performed without interruption. The players form a somewhat smaller circle for this exercise.

Ex. 29

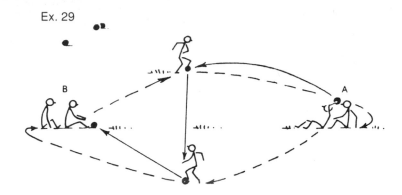

29

Participants 4 - 6 FP

Equipment 1 ball

Description Groups A and B sit across from each other 25 m apart. The first player of group A throws the ball high at a slight angle forward with both hands over his head. He immediately jumps up and sprints toward position B. The first player of group B also jumps up, sprints to the ball and passes it, from the air if possible, into A's running path. A passes directly to the sitting player of group B. Now this player throws the ball over his head with both hands and the exercise begins again.

Objectives 1. Standing up quickly.
2. Improving acceleration speed.
3. Low, direct passing from the air into the teammate's running path.
4. Low, direct passing to a player.

Comments This exercise can be played very well in a gymnasium. The passing will be made easier by the level playing surface. If there are only two players in each group, an improvement of endurance can be achieved through very intensive exercising.

Ex. 30

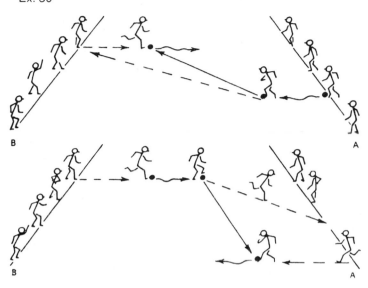

30

Participants 6 - 10 FP

Equipment 1 ball

Description Groups A and B stand across from each other 30 m apart. A player from group A dribbles the ball several steps and calls for a player of group B, who immediately sprints forward. He passes the ball into B's running path and runs to the position that has become free in group B. The player of group B to whom the ball has been passed takes the ball along briefly, calls a player of group A, and passes into his running path. Then he runs to the new free position in group A.

Objectives 1. Strong, low passing into a teammate's running path.
2. Passing and sprinting.
3. Carrying the ball forward with speed.

Comments Make sure that the player called reacts quickly and gets into the open while sprinting. The playing surface between the two groups should be level to make moving the ball forward quickly easier. Demand passing with the outer instep from experienced players.

Ex. 31

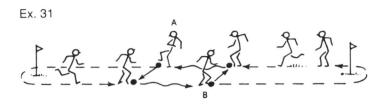

Ex. 32

31
32

Participants   4 - 8 FP

Equipment   1 ball
2 flagstaffs

Description   **Exercise 31:** Set up the flagstaffs about 25 m apart. Both groups A and B stand in front of these staffs. The first player of group A dribbles the ball toward group B; the first player of group B runs toward him. When they meet, A passes the ball into B's running path. B takes it along quickly and passes it into the path of the second group A player who is running toward him. After passing, every player runs to the end of the other group around the flagstaff.

Exercise 32: Set up the flagstaffs about 15 m apart. Groups A and B stand across from each other 3 m apart. They head the ball to each other. After every pass they sprint around the flagstaffs to the end of their group.

Objectives   1. Accurate passing into a teammate's running path.
2. Moving the ball forward quickly.
3. Accurate heading (Exercise 32).
4. Passing and springting.
5. Building endurance.

Comments   The distances between the flagstaffs can be varied. The greater the distance, the more running performance is demanded. In the introductory part of the training session this exercise is used with less intensive exercising to get used to the ball.

Ex. 33

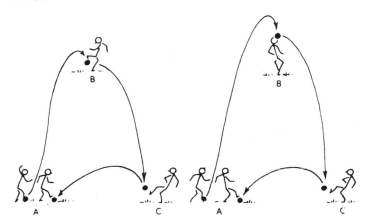

33

Participants   3 FP = one group
Several groups can practise at the same time.

Equipment   1 ball for each group

Description   The players form a triangle. The distances are:
from A to B = about 20 m
from A to C = about 10 m
from B to C = about 15 m
Player A centre-passes the resting ball high to B, who passes it
directly from the air to C. Player C passes the ball in the air to A.
Player A blocks the ball and centre-passes it once more to B, who
passes it either with the foot or head from the air to C.

Objectives   1. Accurate passing to a player.
2. Passing the ball directly.

Comments   After a previously determined number of passes, the positions are
changed. Advanced players are free to pass the ball by whatever
means is quickest.

Ex. 34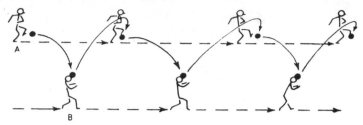

Ex. 35

34
35

Participants   2 FP = one group
              Up to eight groups can play in sequence.

Equipment   1 ball for each group

Description   **Exercise 34:** The distance from A to B is about 3 m. Both players
              move toward a specified target while passing the ball high into each
              other's running paths. Player A passes with his foot to B's head, and
              player B heads the ball back to A's foot. The ball may not touch the
              ground.

              Exercise 35: The distance from A to B is about 5 m. Both players
              move toward a specified target and constantly change their posi-
              tions according to the passing. Player A throws the ball to B's head,
              he controls it and juggles it to A's side. Player A runs after B on the
              right. Now B throws the ball to A's head and repeats the same
              sequence.

Objectives   1. Carrying the ball forward with the head.
              2. Juggling while running.
              3. Making a correct position change.
              4. Accurate passing into a teammate's running path.

Comments   These exercises can be used very effectively in the introductory
              part of a training session. If many pairs of players are practising at
              the same time, let them run one following the other on the playing
              field side from baseline to baseline, go to the opposite side of the
              playing field without practising, and then run and practise around a
              field length. The tempo can be varied.

Ex. 36

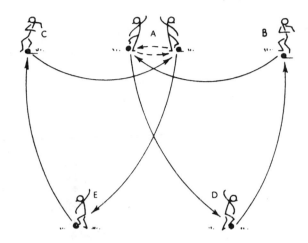

36

Participants   5 FP

Equipment   2 balls

Description   The setup can be seen from the diagram. Players B and C are 10
m apart. The distance from D and E to A is 20 m.
Player C makes a low pass to A who passes the ball half-high to
E. B immediately passes to A. who passes this ball half-high to D.
Players E and D pass their balls back to B and C.

Objectives   1. Accurate passing to a player.
2. Teaching a specific method of kicking. Many variations are
possible.
a. All players make low passes.
b. All players make low passes, except A who passes half high
c. All players pass half high.

Comments   Beginners practise first with stopping. First they pass with the inner
instep, later with the outer instep. The distances are increased for
more advanced players.

Ex. 37

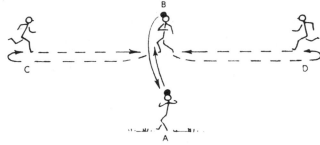

Ex. 38

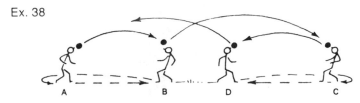

37
38

Participants	4 FP = one group

Several groups can practise at the same time.

Equipment	1 ball

Description   **Exercise 37:** Players B, C and D line up 5 m apart. Player A stands across from player B, 5 m away. Player A heads to B, who immediately heads back and sprints to C or D. Player C or D immediately runs to the middle where he heads back the ball headed to him by A. He then runs to another side position.

Exercise 38: The players line up with A facing B, and C facing D. The distance from A to B and C to D is about 5 m. Players B and D stand with their backs to each other 2 m apart. Player A heads to B, who heads backwards to C. A and B immediately change places. and player C heads to D, who heads backwards to player B, who is now in position A. Players C and D then change places.

Objectives   1. Accurate heading.
2. Passing and sprinting.

Comments   This is a very good exercise for the introductory part of a training session. In this exercise the distance between the players should not be too large: this will enable them to reach the ball passed to them without sprinting.

Ex. 39

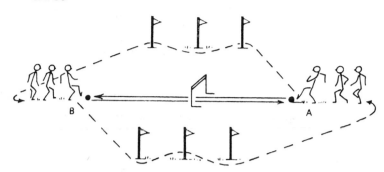

39

Participants 4 - 8 FP

Equipment   1 ball
             1 hurdle
             6 flagstaffs

Description Set up two rows of flagstaffs about 6 m apart. The distance
             between the flagstaffs in the rows is 2 m. Place the hurdle the
             same level as the middle staff and exactly between both rows.
             Groups A and B stand across from each other 4 m from the hurdle.
             The first player of group A passes through the hurdle to B and
             immediately runs through the row of flagstaffs on his right to group
             B. The first player of group B passes directly back through the
             hurdle to group A and immediately runs in slalom through the
             flagstaffs on his right to group A. The second player of group A now
             passes immediately back to group B.

Objectives   1. Direct, low pass to a player.
             2. Passing and sprinting.

Comments   A good playing surface is required to avoid unnecessary interrup-
             tions. Endurance is improved with intensive exercising, and espe-
             cially when each group consists of only two players.

Ex. 40

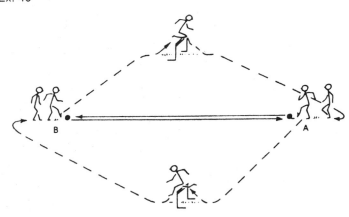

40

Participants   4 - 8 FP

Equipment   1 ball
2 hurdles

Description   Set up two hurdles about 6 m apart. Groups A and B stand facing each other 10 m apart. The first player of group A passes low to B and immediately runs to the hurdle on his left, jumps over it and sprints to the end of group B. The first player of group B makes a low pass to group A and immediately runs to the hurdle on his left, jumps over it and sprints to the end of group A.

Objectives   1. Accurate, direct, low passing to a player.
2. Passing and sprinting.

Comments   A good playing surface is needed to avoid unnecessary interruptions. Endurance is improved with intensive exercising, especially when each group consists of only two players. The hurdles must be set at at least 110 cm to teach jumping ability.

Ex. 41

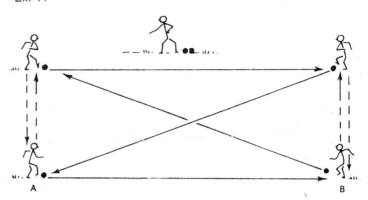

41

Participants   2 FP = one group
              Several groups can practise at the same time.

Equipment   1 ball for each group

Description   The players stand facing each other 10 m apart. Player A makes a
              low pass to B and immediately runs to the left. Player B passes the
              ball directly into A's running path and runs right, where A passes
              directly to him. Now A runs back to his starting position. Player B
              passes directly back to A and also runs back to his own starting
              position. The exercise then begins again without interruption.

Objectives   1. Accurate, low passing.
              2. Passing and sprinting to the side.
              3. Improving endurance.

Comments   This exercise can be employed very effectively in the introductory
              part of a training session. At that time, the movements are not as
              intensive.

Ex. 42

42

Participants   3 FP = one group
Several groups can practise beside each other.

Equipment   1 ball for each group
3 hurdles for each group

Description   Set up the hurdles about 10 m apart in a triangle. A player stands
behind each hurdle. Player A heads the ball gently over the hurdle,
jumps after it and passes it after the first bounce, from the air to
player B's head. Player B controls the ball with his head, heads it
over the hurdle. jumps after it, and passes it after the first bounce
gently to player C's head. C also controls the ball with his head,
heads it over the hurdle, and passes it to A. Each player jumps back
over the hurdle to his starting position after passing.

Objectives   1. Positioning the ball precisely with the head.
2. Accurate. gentle passing to a player.
3. Correct ball control with the head.

Comments   For less experienced players hurdles should not be used at first.
This exercise is excellent for improving a player's feel for the ball
and should be used in training often. The hurdles are set higher to
train jumping ability.

Ex. 43

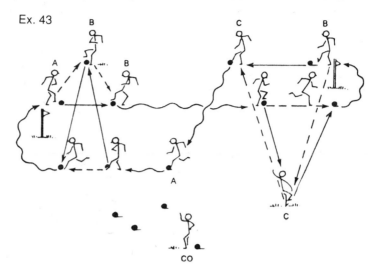

43

Participants 3 FP = one group
Several groups can play at the same time.

Equipment 1 ball for each group
2 flagstaffs for each group

Description Set the two flagstaffs about 30 m apart. The space between each
player is 10 m. Player A dribbles the ball a few metres and then
makes a low, strong pass to player B, who lets it rebound directly
into A's running path. Player A moves the ball forward quickly and
dribbles it around the flagstaff. Player B moves into the open for a
long pass. A makes a low pass into B's running path and sprints to
B's starting position. Player B carries the ball forward quickly,
makes a strong, low pass to C and sprints farther. Player C lets the
ball rebound into B's running path. B moves the ball forward quickly
and dribbles it around the flagstaff. Now player C moves into the
open for a long pass. Player B passes the ball into C's running path
and immediately goes to C's starting position. Player C moves the
ball forward and dribbles it to A's starting position. The exercise
begins again without interruption.

Objectives 1. Training the wall pass.
2. Fast dribbling.
3. Moving into the open at the right moment.
4. Passing and sprinting.

Comments Pay close attention to the moves described for the wall pass on
page 10, Volume 1.

Ex. 44

Ex. 45

44
45

Participants   Any number

Equipment   1 ball for each player

Description   **Exercise 44:** The player juggles the ball with his head. He heads it intermittently as high as he can, does a push-up, and then controls the falling ball with his head and keeps on juggling the ball.

Exercise 45: The player juggles the ball with his feet. Every so often he kicks the ball about 5 m high, does a push-up, controls the falling ball with his foot and keeps on juggling the ball.

Objectives   1. Improving feel for the ball.
2. Improving agility.

Comments   Both exercises should be used mainly in the introductory part of the training session. The following variations are also recommended:
a. sit down;
b. forward roll;
c. backward roll.

Ex. 46

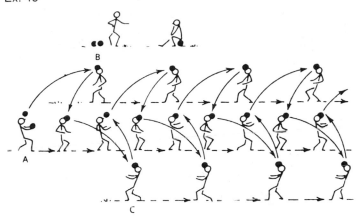

46

Participants 3 FP = one group
Several groups can practise beside each other or in sequence.

Equipment 1 ball for each group

Description Player A stands facing players B and C, about 5 m away. The distance between B and C is about 8 m. Player A heads to B and runs a few steps forward. Player B immediately heads back into A's running path. Player A now heads directly back to player C, who is running backwards, and runs forward. Player C heads into A's running path. A heads the ball back to player B who is running backwards. All three players move back to a previously determined point.

Objectives 1. Gentle passing with the head into a teammate's running path.
2. Passing and running.

Comments This exercise can be used very effectively in the introductory part of a training session. It improves feel for the ball. If many groups are practising at the same time, they should run on the playing field side from baseline to baseline, go to the other playing field side without practising, and then run and practise over a distance of field-length.

Ex. 47   Ex. 48

Ex. 49

Ex. 50

47
48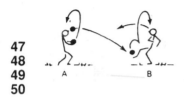
49
50

Participants   2 FP = one group
               Several groups can practise at the same time.

Equipment   1 ball for each group

Description   **Exercise 47:** The players stand facing each other at a distance of
               about 8 m. They pass the ball from the air with their feet. The ball
               is controlled with the thigh and then passed back with the foot.

               Exercise 48: Set up as in Exercise 47. Player A throws or heads
               the ball to B, who controls it with his foot, juggles a few metres
               forward, plays the ball to his head and heads it back to A.

               Exercise 49: Set up as in Exercise 47. The ball is headed to the
               partner's foot. He passes it from his foot to his knee to his head,
               and heads it back.

               Exercise 50: Set up as in Exercise 47. Both players head to each
               other from a jump. The ball headed strongly to the ground is laid
               on for the head with the foot.

Objectives   1. Gentle passing to a player.
               2. Ball control with the left foot and the right foot.

Comments   All the exercises serve mainly to increase the players' feel for the
               ball. They can be used very effectively in the introductory part of the
               training session. Advanced players run to a new position after every
               pass. Both partners then move to a previously determined point:
               one runs forward. the other backward.

Ex. 51

Ex. 52

51
52

Participants 4 - 8 FP

Equipment 1 ball

Description **Exercise 51:** Groups A and B stand facing each other about 10 m apart. The ball is continuously passed low. After the pass, the player runs to the other group.

Exercise 52: Set up as in exercise 51. The first player of group A makes a low pass to B, who controls the ball with a turn, dribbles around his own group, and makes a low pass back to A. Then A controls the ball with a turn, dribbles it around his own group, and makes a low pass back to B. After the pass, the players go to the end of their groups.

Objectives 1. Low passing to a player.
2. Moving the ball forward while turning with the ball (Exercise 52).
3. Fast dribbling.

Comments If the passing is to be done without interruption, the playing surface between the two groups must be level. In Exercise 52, advanced players run to the ball.

Ex. 53   Ex. 54

53
54

Participants   2 FP = one group
Several groups can practise at the same time.

Equipment   1 ball for each group

Description   **Exercise 53:** The players stand facing each other, 5 m apart. Player A throws the ball high to B, who controls it with his head, heads once in between and passes back to A's position. A runs around B after the pass and blocks the ball when it first touches the ground.

Exercise 54: Set up as in Exercise 53. Player A passes the ball gently with his foot to B, who controls it with his foot, plays it to the knee, and from the knee to the head, lets it fall back to his foot and passes it back to his partner. After the pass, A sprints around B and controls the ball with his foot in the air. Now B runs around A while A plays the ball as previously mentioned, before passing back to B.

Objectives   1. Gentle passing.
2. Controlling the ball with the right and left foot.
3. Passing and sprinting.

Comments   These exercises primarily serve to increase the feel for the ball. They can be used effectively in the introductory part of a training session. The distance between the players should be reduced in this case, so that players do not have to sprint around their partners and can run at a moderate pace.

Ex. 55

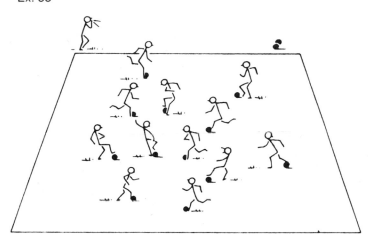

55

Participants   10 - 20 FP

Equipment   1 ball for each player

Description   In a square 15 x 15 m, the players dribble the ball all around, turning frequently. While dribbling, the players must be constantly aware of their surroundings and be prepared to react to the movements of the other players.

Objectives   1. Dribbling the ball at different speeds.
2. Holding the head high while dribbling.
3. Improving hip flexibility through frequent turns while dribbling.

Comments   The size of the playing field depends on the number of players. The field should not be too large. The players must be made to dribble the ball safely in as small a space as possible while keeping it under control. If there are many players, the field between the penalty area and boundary line will serve the purpose well and need not be marked off.
In order to achieve the maximum level of intensity, the players should dribble the ball at the highest tempo possible with the corresponding turns for one minute, and then dribble one minute walking. These movements may be alternated two to five times.

Ex. 56

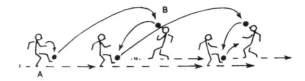

Ex. 57

56
57

Participants   2 FP = one group

Equipment   1 ball for each group

Description   **Exercise 56:** The players A and B stand facing each other about 5 m apart. Player A plays the ball high with his foot to B and goes a few steps forward. Player B heads the ball to A's new position and immediately runs a few steps back. Player A plays the ball directly from the air back to player B. Both players move back to a previously determined point.

Exercise 57: As in Exercise 56, but now both players head the ball. Player A heads with both feet on the ground and B heads from a jump.

Objectives   1. Gentle passing to a player.
2. Passing and sprinting.

Comments   The ball is played accurately and gently, and may not touch the ground. Both exercises are appropriate for the introductory part of a training session, when the pass and the immediate run to a new position need not be stressed heavily and the running is therefore less intensive.

Ex. 58   Ex. 59

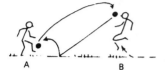   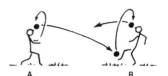

58
59

Participants   2 FP = one group
                Several groups can practise at the same time.

Equipment   1 ball for each group

Description   **Exercise 58:** The players stand facing each other about 8 m apart.
                Player A plays the ball high to B, who heads it powerfully to the
                ground from a jump. A plays the ball high from the air back to B.

                Exercise 59: Set up as in Exercise 58. Player A heads the ball
                gently to player B's foot. B immediately lays the ball on and gently
                passes it to A's foot.

Objectives   1. Gentle passing to a player.
                2. Mastering a powerful header downward from a jump.

Comments   Both exercises serve primarily to increase feel for the ball. They
                can be used very effectively in the introductory part of the training
                session, when headers downward need not be carried out as
                powerfully as they would otherwise have to be.

Ex. 60

Ex. 61

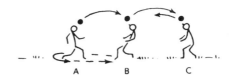

60
61

Participants   3 FP = one group
Several groups can practise at the same time.

Equipment   1 ball for each group

Description   **Exercise 60:** Players A and B stand facing each other at a distance of about 5 m. Player C stands behind A.
Player A heads the ball gently to B and sprints to B's position. Player B heads to C and sprints to C's position. Player C heads to A and sprints to A's present position.

Exercise 61: Players A and B stand facing each other 5 m apart. Player C is 5 m behind B. Player A heads the ball to B, who heads the ball back to C. Players A and B have exchanged positions after the pass. Player C now heads to A, who is now in position B. Player A heads the ball back to B. After the pass, A and C change positions.

Objectives   1. Making a gentle header to a player.
2. Passing and sprinting.

Comments   Both exercises serve primarily to increase feel for the ball. They can be used very effectively in the introductory part of a training session. To develop endurance, the distances may be increased for advanced players.

Ex. 62

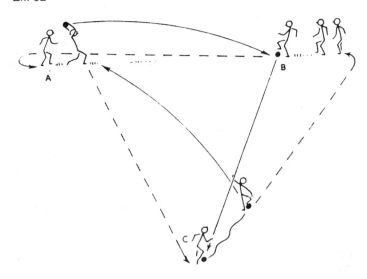

62

Participants   3 - 6 FP

Equipment   1 ball

Description   The three groups form a triangle. The distance from A to B is about 20 m, from C to A and B, about 25 m. Player A throws the ball with both hands over his head to the player who js running toward the ball, who passes it directly from the air to C. Player C takes the ball along and centre-passes to position A. All players change positions in a counter-clockwise direction after passing.

Objectives   1. Making a long, accurate throw-in to a player.
2. Direct passing from the air.
3. Accurate passing to a player.
4. Moving the ball forward quickly.
5. Accurate centre-passing to a player.
6. Passing and sprinting.

Comments   To complete the exercise quickly, group B should have at least 2 players. With 4 FP, good training endurance can be achieved.

Ex. 63

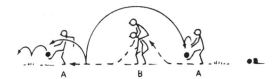

Ex. 64

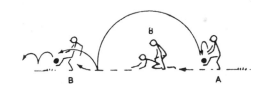

63
64

Participants   2 FP = one group
Several groups can practise at the same time.

Equipment   1 ball for every group

Description   **Exercise 63:** Player B takes a light stride position, supports his hands on his knees, and leans his head forward. Player A stands 5 m behind him with the ball. He kicks the ball high over B, sprints forward, jumps over his partner with his legs straddled (vault), controls the ball before it has touched the ground and juggles it several times.

Exercise 64: Player B stands with legs straddled. Player A stands 5 m behind him with the ball. He kicks the ball high over B, sprints forward, crawls through his partner's straddled legs, controls the ball before it touches the ground twice and juggles it a few times.

Objectives   1. Improving feel for the ball.
2. Improving agility.

Comments   This exercise can be combined effectively with a goal shot. Group A then consists of several players and player B stays in his position until all players of group A have shot on the goal. If this game is used in the introductory part of the training session, the goal shot is excluded and the players practise alternately.

Ex. 65

Ex. 66

65
66

Participants   Any number

Equipment   1 ball for each player

Description   **Exercise 65:** From a back position, the player throws the ball almost straight up into the air with both hands from the chest, jumps up quickly, controls the ball with his foot before it touches the ground, and juggles it a few times.

Exercise 66: The player sits on the ground and throws the ball straight up into the air with both hands. As soon as the ball has left his hands, he jumps up quickly, controls the ball with his head, and juggles it a few more times.

Objectives   1. Getting used to the ball.
2. Improving agility.

Comments   This exercise can be used effectively in the introductory part of the training session. Be sure that the ball is controlled gently after the throw, and does not fall to the ground. Advanced players may control the ball from a jump.

Ex. 67

67

Participants   5 - 10 FP

Equipment   1 ball

Description   A large circle is formed. The central circle of the soccer pitch will serve the purpose well. A player with the ball stands in the middle. He makes a low, strong pass to a player and immediately sprints to another, who leaves his place and sprints to the middle of the circle. The player who is passed to lets the ball rebound gently to the middle of the circle. The new player in the middle of the circle makes a low, strong pass to any partner. He then runs to another player.

Objectives   1. Accurate, strong, low passing to a player.
2. Passing and sprinting.
3. Letting the ball rebound gently.
4. Leaving position immediately when the middle man runs to it.

Comments   Look for a good playing surface to avoid interruptions. Less experienced players may be required first to stop the ball during this exercise. Experienced players may be required to pass the ball with the outer instep.

Ex. 68

Ex. 69

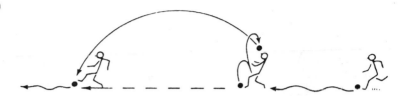

68
69

Participants   Any number

Equipment   1 ball for each player

Description   **Exercise 68:** The player dribbles the ball a few metres at a slow run. In one quick motion he passes the ball far enough forward that he must sprint about 10 m to reach it again. He brings the ball under control quickly and returns gradually to a slow running tempo.

Exercise 69: The player dribbles the ball a few metres at a slow run. Again, he quickly stops the ball, kicks it from his foot to his knee, passes it from his knee to his head, and then heads it far forward. He runs after the the ball, quickly brings it under control, and gradually returns to a slow run.

Objectives   1. Passing and sprinting.
2. Taking the ball along quickly.
3. Rhythm change.

Comments   The players practise on the playing field side from baseline to baseline, go without practising to the other playing field side, and practise further a whole length of the soccer pitch. Endurance training is the main feature of this exercise.

Ex. 70   Ex. 71

Ex. 72   Ex. 73

70
71
72
73

Participants   Any number

Equipment   1 ball for each player

Description   **Exercise 70:** The player juggles the ball with both feet, from a sitting position.

Exercise 71: The player clamps the ball between his feet, jumps while bringing his knees high into a crouch position, swings his calves forward and lets go of the ball. Just before the ball hits the ground for the first time, the ball is controlled in the air and juggled a few times.

Exercise 72: As in Exercise 71. The player jumps high and, while swinging his legs backward, the ball is thrown over his head. The player controls it before it bounces once and juggles it.

Exercise 73: The sitting player throws the ball with both hands over his head onto the ground. He jumps up quickly, controls the ball with his head and juggles it a few times.

Objectives   1. Improving feel for the ball.
2. Improving agility.

Comments   All exercises should be used mainly in the introductory part of a training session.

Ex. 74

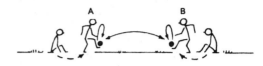

Ex. 75

Ex. 76

74
75
76

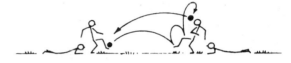

Participants 2 FP = one group

Equipment 1 ball for each group

Description **Exercise 74:** Players A and B stand facing each other 3 m apart. The ball is passed high to the partner who controls it in the air and juggles it once before passing it back. After passing, each player quickly sits down and stands up again.

Exercise 75: As in Exercise 74. The ball is now passed with the head.

Exercise 76: Set up as in Exercise 74. The ball is headed to the partner. The partner controls the ball with his foot and and bounces it up to the knee, and from the knee to the head. After passing, each player lies down and immediately stands up again.

Objectives 1. Gentle passing to a player.
2. Controlling the ball with the left and right foot.
3. Training of agility.

Comments All exercises serve primarily to improve feel for the ball. They can be used effectively in the introductory part of the training session.

Ex. 77

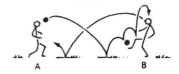

Ex. 78

Ex. 79

77
78
79

Participants   2 FP = one group
Several groups can practise at the same time.

Equipment   1 ball for each group

Description   **Exercise 77:** Players A and B stand opposite each other about 8 m apart. Player A heads the ball to B so that it reaches him after bouncing once. Player B controls the ball with his foot, juggles it to his knee and from there to his head, and heads the ball back to A. The ball must reach A after bouncing once.

Exercise 78: Set up as in Exercise 77. Player A now passes with his foot. The ball must reach B after bouncing once. Player B controls the ball with his foot, bounces it to his chest and then lets it fall to his calf. He passes with the calf to A so that the ball reaches A after bouncing once.

Exercise 79: Set up as in Exercise 77. The ball is passed so that it reaches the partner after one bounce. It is controlled with his foot, passed onto the thigh and hit back to the partner with the thigh.

Objectives   1. Gentle passing to a player.
2. Ball control with the left and right foot.

Comments: All exercises serve primarily to increase the feel for the ball. They can be used effectively in the introductory part of the training session. The distance between the partners is increased for advanced players.

Ex. 80

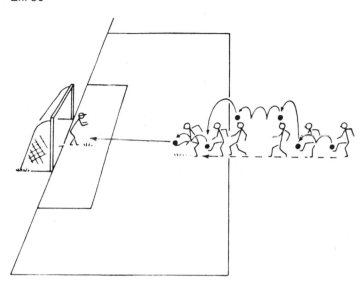

80

Participants   1 - 8 FP

Equipment   1 ball for each player

Description   The players stand each with his own ball, 40 m from the goal. They
              juggle the ball a few metres with the foot, pass it high to the head,
              juggle a few metres with the head, then again with the foot until they
              reach the penalty area. On the penalty area boundary, a positioned
              shot at the goal from the air is made.

Objectives   1. Improving feel for the ball.
              2. Aiming volley shot at the goal.
              3. Following up the goal shot.

Commments   Each player sprints to fetch the ball, dribbles it quickly back to the
              starting position and goes to end of the group.
              If this exercise is used in the introductory part of the training
              session, the sprint is left out. The player runs to the ball and slowly
              dribbles it back to the starting position.

Ex. 81

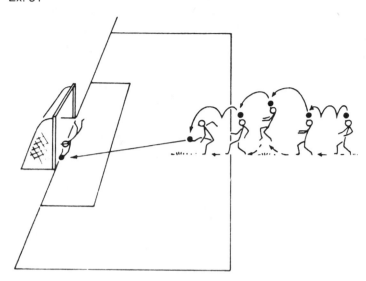

81

Participants   1 - 8 FP

Equipment   1 ball for each player

Description   The players stand each with one ball about 40 m away from the goal. Each juggles the ball with his head to the goal. In between, the ball is headed somewhat higher than usual and the ball is gently controlled with the head from a jump and then juggled farther. At the penalty area boundary, a positioned goal shot is made from the air.

Objectives   1. Improving feel for the ball.
2. Making positioned volley shot at the goal.
3. Following up the goal shot.

Comments   Each player sprints to fetch the ball he has shot at the goal, dribbles it quickly back to the starting position and goes to the end of the group.

Ex. 82

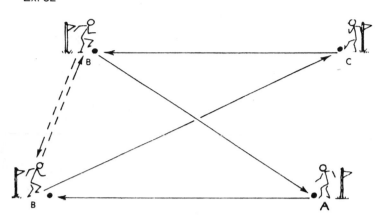

82

Participants   3 FP = one group
               Several groups can practise at the same time.

Equipment   1 ball for each group
               4 flagstaffs

Description   Set up the flagstaffs to form a rectangle. The distance from A to B
               is about 15 m, from A to C about 10 m.
               Player A passes the ball low to B, who passes it directly to C and
               runs to the free flagstaff. Player C passes directly there. Now player
               B passes to A and runs back to his starting position. While A and C
               keep their positions, player B goes back and forth between the two
               flagstaffs until the CO calls for a position change.

Objectives   1. Passing and sprinting.
               2. Accurate, low passing to a player.
               3. Direct passing.

Comments   It is useful to require player B to make a strong pass to A and C,
               while they let the passed ball rebound gently back. Less experi-
               enced players may stop the ball before passing.

Ex. 83

Ex. 84

83
84

Participants   2 FP = one group
Several groups can practise at the same time.

Equipment   1 ball for each group
1 flagstaff for each group

Description   **Exercise 83:** Players A and B stand facing each other about 8 m apart. A flagstaff is set up about 3 m behind player B. Player B passes with his foot to A so that the ball bounces once before reaching the partner. Player A controls the ball in the air, juggles it once and passes the ball in the same way back to B so that, after he has run around the flagstaff, the ball reaches him after one bounce.

Exercise 84: Set up as in Exercise 83. Player A throws the ball high to B. He heads it back to A and immediately sprints around the flagstaff. A immediately throws the ball to B again.

Objectives   1. Passing and sprinting.
2. Improving feel for the ball.

Comments   If the distance from B to the flagstaff is increased, this exercise will improve endurance. The positions may be reversed after several cycles of the exercise have been completed.

Ex. 85

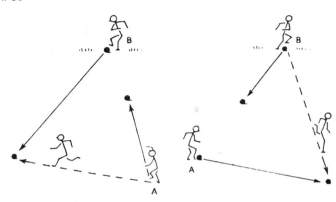

85

Participants 2 FP = one group
Several groups can practise at the same time.

Equipment 1 ball for each player

Description Players A and B each dribble the ball at a slow run while observing the other's movements. In a single movement, A passes to B and runs into the open, sprinting in any direction. Player B immediately passes his ball into A's running path and then controls the ball from A. Both players now dribble the balls they have exchanged at a slow run, again, mindful of each other's movements. Now player B begins with the pass first and sprints into the open.

Objectives 1. Observing a teammate while dribbling.
2. Passing and sprinting.
3. Training reaction ability.

Comments To train reaction ability, the coach should not allow the players to dribble the ball more than 5 m from each other. However, if the intention is to improve running speed, the distances between the players can be made greater.

Ex. 86

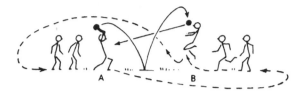

Ex. 87

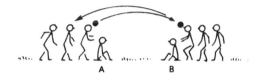

86
87

Participants 4 - 8 FP = one team
2 - 3 teams may practise at the same time.

Equipment 1 ball for each team

Description **Exercise 86:** Groups A and B form a team. The first players of the groups stand across from each other, approximately 8 m apart. The player from group A throws the ball with both hands powerfully to the ground and runs immediately to the end of group B. The player from group B heads the ball from a jump to the next player of group A and runs immediately to the end of group A.

Exercise 87: As in Exercise 86. The distance between the first player of each group is 3 m. The players of group A and B head the ball down the line and sit on the ground after the pass. All players sit until the last one of group B; and then after passing in the proper order, the players stand up again, one after the other.

Objectives **Exercise 86:**
1. Accurate heading from a jump.
2. Passing and sprinting.

Exercise 87
1. Improving feel for the ball.

Comments The teams may compete with each other. The team to return the starting position first wins.

Ex. 88

Ex. 89

88
89

Participants   Any number

Equipment   1 ball for each player

Description   **Exercise 88:** The players run with the ball to a specified point while juggling the ball alternately from foot to head and from head to foot. The ball may only be touched once at the head and at the foot.

Exercise 89: As in Exercise 88. The ball is only juggled with the foot. Every so often, it is played higher than usual, controlled again from a jump and juggled farther.

Objectives   1. Improving feel for the ball.
2. Training concentration.

Comments   This exercise should be used mainly in the introductory part of the training session. If it is combined with a goal shot, the goal shot should be positioned from the air with minimum effort.

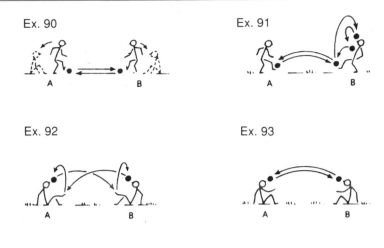

Ex. 90   Ex. 91

Ex. 92   Ex. 93

90
91
92
93

Participants 2 FP = one group
Several groups can practise at the same time.

Equipment 1 ball for each group

Description **Exercise 90:** Players A and B stand facing each other, 5 m apart. They make a direct, low pass to each other. After each pass, the player sits and stands in one quick motion.

Exercise 91: Set up as in Exercise 90. The partners pass the ball to each other with the foot from the air. After the pass, each player juggles the ball from his foot to his head and back down over the chest to the foot.

Exercise 92: Players A and B sit across from each other about 2 m apart. Player A hits the ball with his head to B's foot. Player B passes the ball directly from his foot to his head and heads back to A's foot. Players should aim at an uninterrupted practice of this exercise.

Exercise 93: Starting position as in Exercise 92. The ball is headed continuously from one seated player to the other.

Objectives 1. Improving feel for the ball.
2. Training concentration.

Comments These exercises should be used mainly in the introductory part of the training session. It may be useful to introduce running exercises for the players between these exercises.

Ex. 94

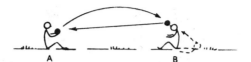

Ex. 95

94
95

Participants   2 FP = one group
Several groups can practise at the same time.

Equipment   1 ball for each group

Description   **Exercise 94:** The players sit facing each other about 5 m apart. Player A throws the ball with both hands in an arc to B, who brings his upper body forward from far back and powerfully heads back to A. After a set of ten balls, the players change positions.

Exercise 95: The players sit facing each other, 3 m apart. Player A throws the ball high and heads it to B, who controls it with his foot and kicks it to his hand. Now B passes the ball as A has done.

Objectives   1. Improving feel for the ball.
2. Training agility.

Comments   With advanced players, the distance between the two players is increased. The two exercises should never be assigned in succession: use running exercises to move from one to the other.

Ex. 96

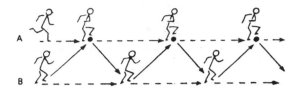

Ex. 97

96
97

Participants   2 FP = one group
              Several groups may practise in sequence.

Equipment   I ball for each group

Description   **Exercise 96:** The distance from A to B is about 5 m. Both players
              move toward a specific goal while making direct low passes into the
              other's running path.

              Exercise 97: As in Exercise 96. The ball is passed half-high so that
              it reaches the partner after bouncing once.

Objectives   1. Accurate passing into a teammate's running path.
              2. Passing and sprinting forward.

Comments   If there are many pairs of players. the coach may have them run and
              practise on the playing field side from baseline to baseline, go to the
              other side without practising. run around the playing field line, and
              begin practising again. The tempo can be varied. These exercises
              may be used effectively in the introductory part of the training
              session.

Ex. 98

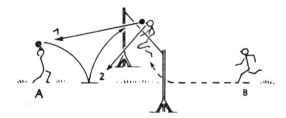

98

Participants 2 FP

Equipment 1 ball
2 high jump stands with a rope

Description The rope is stretched about 2 m high, depending on the height of the players. These players stand facing each other, about 10 m apart. The stands are set between them. Player A throws the ball with both hands powerfully to the ground. The ball must just clear the line after bouncing up. Player B runs to the ball and heads it from a jump over the line back to A. B runs immediately back to his starting position and A throws again.

Objectives 1. Running up and jumping in a three-step rhythm.
2. Powerful heading.
3. Improving jumping ability.

Comments For defenders, the CO has the ball headed into the raised arms of the partner, but for forwards, down toward the ground. After a set of ten jumps, the partners change positions.

Ex. 99

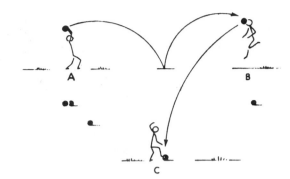

99

Participants 3 FP = one group
Several groups can practise at the same time.

Equipment 1 ball for each group

Description The players form a triangle. The distance between the players is about 10 m.
Player A throws the ball forcefully with both hands to the ground. Player B heads from a jump to C, who controls the ball and throws it to the ground with both hands. Player A heads from a jump to B. Now B throws to C and he heads to A.

Objectives 1. Heading accurately from a jump.
2. Heading downward forcefully.

Comments With advanced players, C presents himself left and right for a header pass. The ball is now headed by B into C's running path. The distance between the players may be increased, so that the players must sprint toward the ball to be able to head it from a jump to their partners.

Drills for Team and Group Practice

Ex. 100

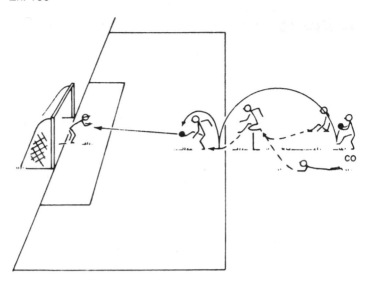

100

Participants   1 - 5 FP   1 GK

Equipment   1 ball for each player
1 hurdle

Description   Set up a hurdle about 25 m in front of the goal. The coach stands with the balls 35 m away from the goal. The players stand, lay, or sit left or right of the CO.
The coach shoots the ball in an arc over the hurdle. The player must immediately jump after it and shoot it from the air at the goal before it has touched the ground twice.

Objectives   1. Improvement of acceleration speed.
2. Improving of agility.
3. Improving of jumping ability.
4. Practising shot at the goal.
5. Following up the goal shot.

Comments   If the improvement of jumping ability is the most important objective, the hurdle should be raised as high as possible. The volley shot should be positioned and need not be done with full strength.

Ex. 101

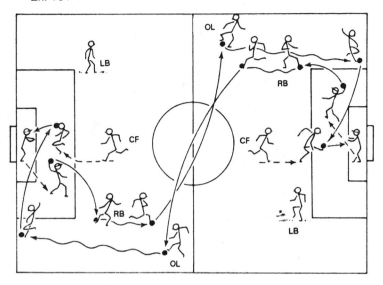

101

Participants   2 GK   2 - 4 FB   2 - 4 WF   2 CF

Equipment   4 balls

Description   The starting positions can be seen from the diagram.
The GK throws the ball to the RB (right back), who takes it along
briefly, passes half high to OL (outside left) in the other playing field
side. The OL move the ball forward quickly, dribbles it, changing
tempo, to the baseline, and centre-passes it to the CF, who has just
run to that position. He shoots at the goal from the air. The same
game move is now made in the opposite direction. If there are two
FB and two WF on each playing field side, then the GK throws the
ball alternately to the RB and the LB. The LB then passes far to the
OR.

Objectives   1. Accurate throwing-out.
2. Carrying the ball forward quickly.
3. Long, diagonal, accurate passing into a teammate's running
path.
4. Moving the ball forward quickly.
5. Dribbling the ball at constantly changing speed.
6. Accurate centre-passing.
7. Positioning oneself at the right moment.
8. Shooting directly on goal.

Ex. 102

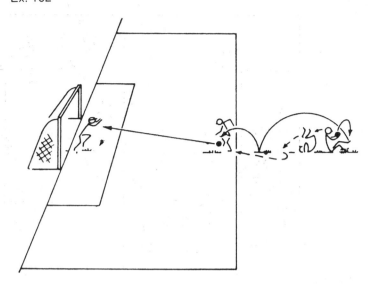

102

Participants 1 - 8 FP 1 GK

Equipment   1 ball for each player

Description   The player sits with the ball about 25 m in front of the goal. The ball is kicked high over his head. After an immediate backward roll, the player turns and quickly runs to the ball, which he must shoot at the goal before it touches the ground twice.

Objectives   1. Fast backward rolling and turning.
                    2. Improving acceleration.
                    3. Volley shot at the goal.
                    4. Following up the goal shot.

Comments   The player shoots at the goal, sprints to fetch the ball, and goes quickly back to his starting position. The CO pays attention that the players begin one after the other. The FO play in their positions where possible. The WF begin level with the side boundary of the penalty area.

Ex. 103

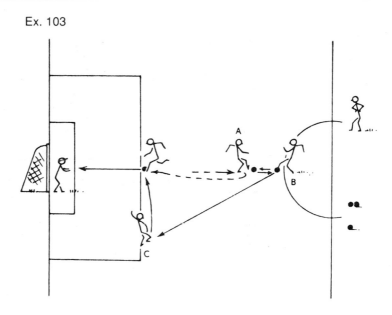

103

Participants A = 1 - 5 FP   B = 1 FP   C = 1 FP   1 GK

Equipment 1 ball for each player of group A

Description Player B stands with the balls in the central circle. Player A stands facing him about 20 m away. Player C stands near the penalty area corner. Player A sprints to B, who immediately makes a low, strong pass to A. Player A lets the ball rebound to B, turns quickly and sprints toward the goal. Player B immediately makes a low, strong pass to C, who passes the ball into A's running path. A shoots directly for the goal.

Objectives 1. Being prepared to accept a pass while sprinting.
2. Strong, low passing to a player.
3. Letting the ball rebound gently.
4. Turning quickly.
5. Direct passing into a teammate's running path.
6. Making direct, strong goal shot while running full speed.
7. Following up the goal shot.

Comments The player shoots at the goal, sprints to fetch the ball, gives it to player B and sits down at the end of group A. Players B and C change positions after a certain number of passes. Pay attention that the passes are strong.

Ex. 104

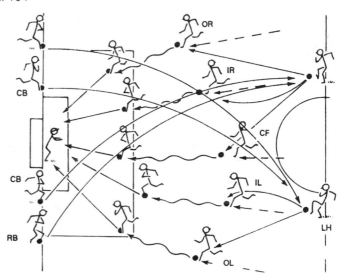

Participants   1 GK   3 - 5 FB   2 - 3 HB   4 - 7 FO

Equipment   1 ball for each player

Description   The FB stand on the baseline, left and right of the goal, with several balls. The FO are about 35 m from the baseline; the HB are on the halfway line or in the other side of the field.
The FB hit the balls, one after the other, to the HB. They control the balls briefly and pass them into the running paths of the FO, who are readying themselves to accept passes while running toward the goal. After moving the ball forward briefly, they shoot at the goal.

Objectives   1. Long, diagonal passing to a player.
2. Correct ball control.
3. Getting into the open at the right moment.
4. Accurate passing into a teammate's running path.
5. Moving the ball forward properly and effectively.
6. Making a strong goal shot while running full speed.

Comments   To have fast and trouble free exercising, the CO calls out the FO he wants ready to accept a pass. The HB must react to this by passing. The GK gives the balls shot at the goal to the FB.

Ex. 105

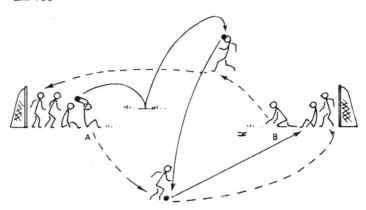

105

Participants   4 - 6 FP

Equipment   1 ball for each player of group A
                2 movable large goals

Description   Groups A and B sit facing each other, 20 m apart. The first player
                of group A throws the ball powerfully forward and sideways to the
                ground with both hands. He jumps up and sprints toward position
                B. The first player of group B also jumps up after A's throw-out, runs
                to the ball, and heads it, if possible from a jump, into player A's
                running path. A plays it directly toward the goal behind group B. The
                players of group B defend the goal.
                Now the first player of group B throws the ball powerfully forward
                and sideways to the ground.

Objectives   1. Standing up quickly.
                2. Improving acceleration.
                3. Accurate passing with the head into a teammate's running path.
                4. Shooting directly into the goal.

Comments   This exercise may be used to improve endurance; no more than
                two players in each group should be used.

Ex. 106

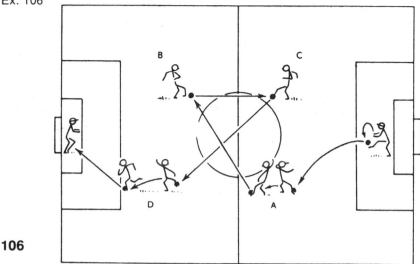

106

Participants   4 FP   2 GK

Equipment   4 balls

Description   The setup may be seen in the diagram. The GK throws or shoots the ball to player A standing near the halfway line. Player A takes the ball along briefly, and passes diagonally to B, who immediately lets the ball rebound to C, who gets ready to accept a pass. Player C moves the ball forward briefly and makes an accurate, half-high diagonal pass into D's running path. After carrying the ball forward briefly, D shoots for the goal. The GK on this side of the playing field now throws or shoots the ball to B, who after moving the ball forward briefly, passes diagonally to A. Player A lets the ball rebound to D, who gets ready to accept a pass. D moves the ball forward, and makes a half-high pass into C's running path. C shoots for the goal.

Objectives   1. Accurate, long passing to a player.
2. Long, half-high, diagonal passing to a player and into a team-mate's running path.
3. Carrying the ball forward quickly.
4. Shooting at the goal while running full speed.

Comments   Two balls are given to each GK. If a shot misses the goal, the GK immediately throws the second ball into the game. Ensure that the pass reaches the teammate quickly, and that he is therefore able to make a strong and accurate shot.

Ex. 107

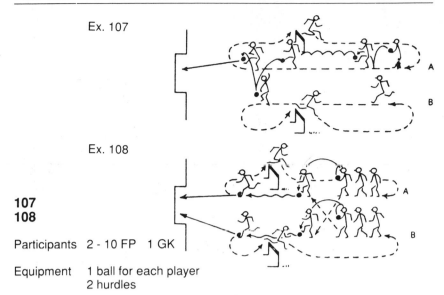

Ex. 108

107
108

Participants 2 - 10 FP   1 GK

Equipment   1 ball for each player
             2 hurdles

Description: **Exercise 107:** Set up the hurdles about 20 m in front of the goal.
             Groups A and B are about 40 m in front of the goal. The distance
             between them is 5 m.
             The first player of group A juggles the ball with his feet until he is 20
             m in front of the goal. At this moment the first player of group B
             sprints forward and gets ready to receive a pass. Player A passes
             the ball half high from the air to B, who deflects directly into A's
             running path. The deflection must be done in such a way that A can
             shoot at the goal directly from the air. After the goal shot, each
             player runs back to his original position, first jumping over the
             hurdle.

             Exercise 108: Set up as in Exercise 107. The first players of groups
             A and B head the ball forward, run diagonally to the partner's ball,
             carry it forward quickly to the goal and shoot in sequence at the goal.
             After the goal shot continue as in Exercise 107.

Objectives   **Exercise 107:** 1. Improving of feel for the ball.
             2. Getting ready to receive a pass.
             3. Accurate, half high passing into a teammate's running path.
             4. Accurate goal shot from the air.

             Exercise 108: 1. Carrying the ball forward quickly.
             2. Making a positioned goal shot after dribbling.

Comments   As in Exercises 118 and 119.

Ex. 109

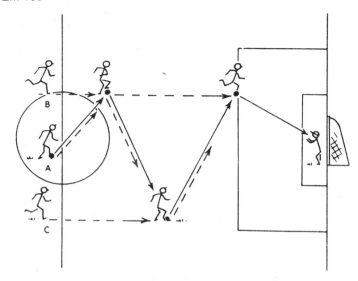

109

Participants   3 - 15 FP   1 GK

Equipment   1 ball for every three players

Description   Groups of three are formed; each group takes up a position on the
halfway line 10 m apart. The middle player makes a strong, low
pass into B's running path and runs after the ball. Player B makes
a direct. low. strong pass to C and sprints to this position. Player C
now passes into A's running path. A, who is now on the left side,
makes a strong. low pass to B, who is now on the right side. The
passing and side changes continue until the penalty area has been
reached. The player who is in possession shoots at the goal from
the penalty area boundary.

Objectives   1. Strong. low passing into a teammate's running path.
2. Passing and sprinting.
3. Running after the passed ball: the position change follows behind
the passed ball.
4. Making a direct goal shot while running full speed.

Comments   If several groups are practising at the same time. the players go
immediately outside the playing zone back to the starting position
after a successful goal shot.
The quality of the exercise very much depends on the condition of
the playing surface.

Ex. 110

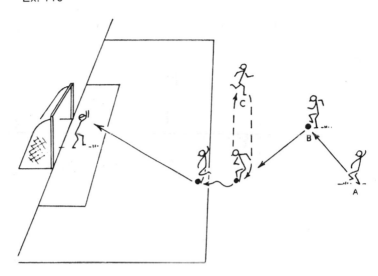

110

Participants   A = 1 FP   B = 1 FP   C = 1 - 5 FP   1 GK

Equipment   1 ball for each player of group C

Description   Player A makes a covered pass to B. C immediately prepares to receive a pass. Player B deflects into C's running path. C moves the ball forward, turning toward the goal; after dribbling the ball briefly, he shoots at the goal.

Objectives   1. Covered passing with the outer instep to a player.
           2. Getting into the open at the right moment.
           3. Correctly letting the ball rebound into a teammate's running path.
           4. Moving the ball forward quickly.
           5. Making a positioned goal shot after fast dribbling.
           6. Following up a goal shot.

Comments   To keep players A and B more intensively occupied, there should be more players in group C. After a certain period, A and B trade places with players in group C. The player who shoots at the goal, sprints to fetch the ball, gives it to player A and runs to the end of group C.

Ex. 111

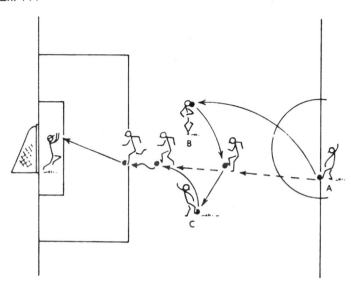

111

Participants   A = 1 - 5 FP   B = 1 FP   C = 1 FP   1 GK

Equipment   1 ball for each player of group A

Description   Player A centre-passes to B's head and sprints forward. Player B heads back into player A's running path. A passes the ball immediately to player C and sprints further. Player C lets the ball rebound into A's running path. A moves it forward and shoots at the goal.

Objectives   1. Accurate, high passing to a player.
2. Passing and sprinting.
3. Making an accurate header into a teammate's running path.
4. Teaching the wall pass.
5. Making a positioned goal shot after fast dribbling.
6. Following up the goal shot.

Comments   See page 10 for the technical and tactical game moves in the wall pass.
The player shoots at the goal, sprints to fetch the ball and dribbles it at a moderate pace back to the starting position.

Ex. 112

Ex. 113

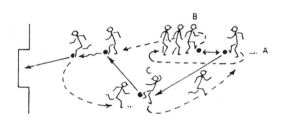

112
113

Participants   A = 1 FP   B = 1 - 5 FP   C = 1 FP   1 GK

Equipment   1 ball for each player of group B

Description   **Exercise 112:** Player A stands about 35 m from the goal. The distance between players A and B is about 3 m. Players A and B pass several times to each other from the air. Suddenly B turns after the pass and sprints to the goal. Player A passes the ball forward directly. Player B takes the ball along, which has bounced up, and shoots at the goal while running full speed.

Exercise 113 Starting position as in Exercise 112. Group C is added. Players A and B now make low passes to each other. When B turns and sprints to the goal, A passes directly to C, who passes directly into player B's running path. Player B carries the ball forward and shoots at the goal while running full speed. He immediately goes to player C's position, C changes to A, and A to B.

Objectives   1. Gentle, direct passing.
2. Accurate passing into a teammate's running path.
3. Moving the ball forward quickly.
4. Making a positioned goal shot after dribbling the ball.

Comments   After a certain time period player A is replaced in Exercise 112. If group B is small, these exercises can be used effectively to improve endurance. Where group B is small, there must be two players in group C.

Ex. 114

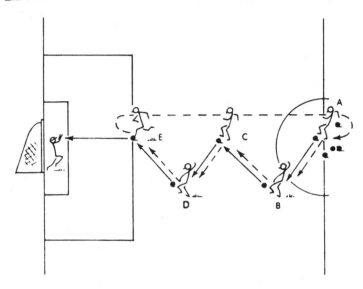

114

Participants   A = 1 - 6 FP   B, C, D, E, = 1 FP each 1 GK

Equipment   1 ball for each player of group A

Description   Player A makes a low, strong pass to B and sprints after the ball to
             B's position. The ball passes from player to player and the positions
             change accordingly. The player at station E shoots for the goal,
             fetches the ball and quickly proceeds to A's starting position.

Objectives   1. Strong, low passing to a player.
             2. Passing and sprinting.
             3. Making a direct goal shot.
             4. Following up the goal shot.

Comments   This exercise is especially good for beginners. To make the
             exercise more intensive, several players are in position A. The next
             player begins the moment player D has the ball.

Ex. 115

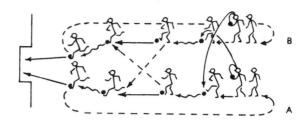

Ex. 116

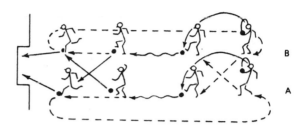

115
116

Participants   2 - 10 FP   1 GK

Equipment   1 ball for every two players

Description **Exercise 115:** Groups A and B stand 40 m away from the goal. The
distance between the two groups is 5 m.
At a command from A, the first players of both groups head their
balls to each other, sprint to their respective balls and quickly. At a
new command from A, the players make a long pass. Each player
runs diagonally to his partner's ball, moves it along quickly and
shoots at the goal from the penalty area. Meanwhile, the next group
has already started.

Exercise 116: As in Exercise 115, but the ball is headed deep and
the players run diagonally. The pass with the foot is made diagonally into the partner's running path.

Objectives   1. Accurate heading.
2. Carrying the ball along quickly.
3. Dribbling briefly.
4. Accurate passing into the teammate's running path.
5. Making a goal shot while running full speed.

Comments   As in Exercise 118 and 119. In addition, the second shooter must
pay special attention to the starting position of the GK. If the GK is
lying down, for example, the player should make the appropriate
shot.

Ex. 117

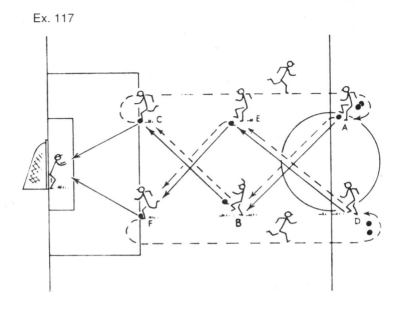

117

Participants   A = 1 - 6 FP   B = 1 FP   C = 1 FP
                  D = 1 - 6 FP   E = 1 FP   F = 1 FP   1 GK

Equipment   1 ball for each player of groups A and D

Description   The players take up positions in the inside right and inside left positions on the halfway line, half way between the halfway line and penalty area, and on the penalty area boundary. Player A passes to B and runs immediately to B's position. Player B passes to C and runs there. Player C shoots at the goal and goes to A's starting position. Players D, E and F pass and run in the same way.

Objectives   1. Accurate, low passing to a player.
              2. Passing and sprinting.
              3. Making a direct goal shot.
              4. Following up the goal shot.

Comments: This exercise is especially suited for less experienced players. The players in positions C and F first fetch the ball shot at the goal and quickly take up positions A and D.

Ex. 118

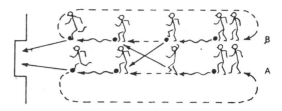

Ex. 119

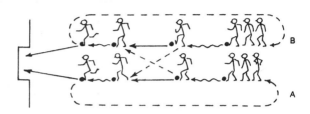

118
119

Participants 2 - 5 FP 1 GK

Equipment 1 ball for each player

Description **Exercise 118:** Groups A and B are 40 m away from the goal. The distance between the groups is 5 m. The first players of these two groups dribble the ball a few metres. On command from player A, they pass the ball into each other's running path, carry the partner's ball a few steps and shoot at the goal from the penalty area boundary while running full speed. The next pair of players should already have started dribbling.

Exercise 119: As in Exercise 118. Both players make a deep pass on A's command. Now the running direction is diagonal.

Objectives 1. Dribbling the ball briefly while watching the partner.
2. Accurate passing into the partner's running path.
3. Moving the ball forward quickly.
4. Making a positioned goal shot after dribbling.

Comments If the number of players is small, building endurance becomes a main point of the exercise. Each player sprints to retrieve the ball he has shot at the goal and runs slowly out of the playing zone to the end of his group. Pay attention that both players do not shoot at the same time.

Ex. 120

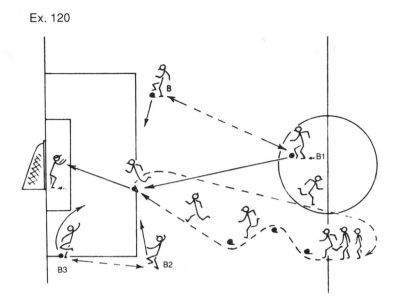

120

Participants   A = 3 - 8 FP   B = 1 FP   1 GK

Equipment   1 ball for each player of group A
3 balls or flagstaffs

Description   The first player of group A sprints in slalom around the balls and then toward the goal. Player B makes a low pass from the centre circle into A's running path. A makes a direct goal shot.

Objectives   1. Accurate passing into a teammate's running path.
2. Making a direct goal shot while running full speed.
3. Building endurance.
4. Following up the goal shot.

Comments   Player B can pass from various positions (see B1 to B3). The change, however, comes after a certain time and is not constant. The players of group A fetch the ball immediately after the goal shot and go to the end of their group. If building endurance is the main purpose, there should be no more than three players in group A. Two players are then alternately assigned as ball fetchers.

Ex. 121

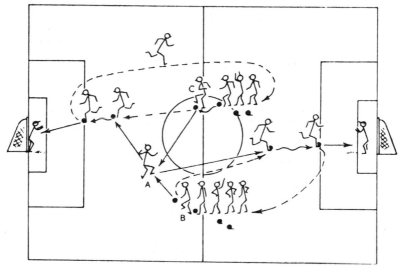

121

Participants   A = 1 FP   B = 2 - 5 FP   C = 2 - 5 FP   1 GK

Equipment   1 ball for each player of groups B and C

Description   The first player of group B makes a low pass to A, turns quickly and sprints toward the goal. Player A passes directly into B's running path. B briefly dribbles the ball and then shoots at the goal. Player A immediately receives a pass from the first of group C. He passes the ball into C's running path. C moves the ball forward briefly, and shoots at the goal. Players B and C go to the end of their groups after fetching the ball shot at the goal.

Objectives   1. Accurate, low passing.
2. Passing and sprinting.
3. Accurate, low passing into a teammate's running path.
4. Moving the ball along quickly.
5. Making a goal shot while running full speed.
6. Building concentration.

Comments   The exercise must be fast-paced to increase player A's concentration. After a certain time, player A is replaced. HB are primarily assigned for this. Player A's position can be moved closer to one or the other goal. In this way, the difference between short and long passes will be more extreme.

Ex. 122

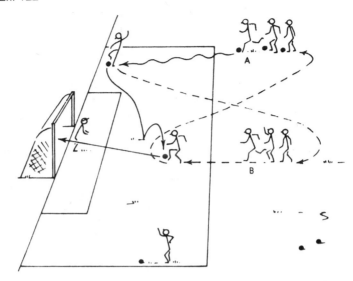

122

Participants 4 - 10 FP   1 GK

Equipment 1 ball for every two players

Description The first player of group A dribbles the ball along the penalty area line close to the baseline and centre-passes to the penalty spot, to which the first player of group B has run. B shoots directly at the goal. Immediately after making the centre pass or goal shot, the player runs to the end of the other group.

Objectives 1. Fast dribbling.
2. Getting into the open at the right moment.
3. Accurate centre pass.
4. Making a direct goal shot from the air.
5. Following up the goal shot.

Comments First player B sprints to fetch the ball he has shot at the goal and dribbles it at a moderate tempo to group A. With beginners, the ball is centre-passed so that it reaches the partner after bouncing once.

Ex. 123

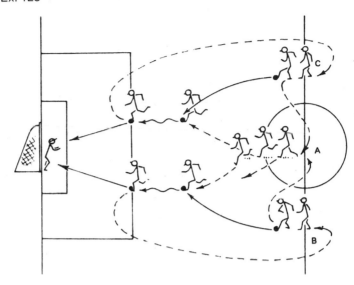

123

Participants   A = 2 - 8 FP   B = 1 FP   C = 1 FP   1 GK

Equipment   1 ball for each player in group A

Description   The first player of group A sprints to the inside left position. There he immediately receives a strong, low pass with the outer instep from the first player of group B, takes the ball along to the goal and shoots at the goal from the penalty area while running full speed. He immediately fetches his ball and goes to the end of group B, while the first player of group B moves to group A.
The next player sprints to the inside right position. He immediately receives a strong, low pass with the outer instep from C. He moves the ball forward to the goal and shoots from the penalty area while running full speed. He immediately fetches his ball and goes to the end of group C, while the player from group C moves to group A.

Objectives   1. Making a covered pass into a teammate's running path.
2. Moving the ball along quickly.
3. Shooting at the goal while running full speed.
4. Building endurance.

Comments   If building endurance is the principle aim, it is recommended that no more than six players be used. Two players are assigned as ball fetchers.

Ex. 124

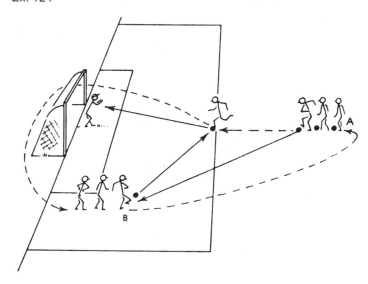

124

Participants   4 - 10 FP   1 GK

Equipment   1 ball for every two players

Description   The first player of group A makes a low, strong pass to B, who is on
the outside right of the goal area. Player B makes a direct, strong
pass back into A's running path. A shoots at the goal without
stopping, continues to run on, fetches the ball, and goes to the end
of group B. Player B goes to the end of group A after passing back
to A.

Objectives   1. Making a strong, low pass to a player.
2. Passing and sprinting.
3. Making a direct, low pass into a teammate's running path.
4. Making a positioned goal shot while running full speed.
5. Following up the goal shot.

Comments   Remember that position changes should be made quickly, and
outside of the playing and shooting zones.
The goal shot should not be made with full strength. Players should
stop and make positioned shots.

Ex. 125

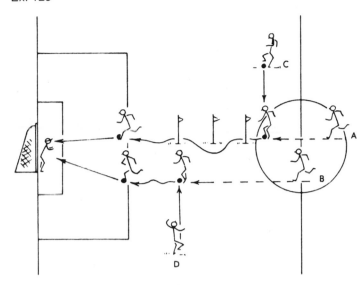

125

Participants   A = 2 - 5 FP   B = 2 - 5 FP   C = 1 FP
              D = 1 FP   1 GK

Equipment   1 ball for each player of groups A and B
              3 flagstaffs

Description   Set up three flagstaffs in the inside right of the field, in a line 8 m
apart, starting 2 m from the goal.
Groups A and B stand on the halfway line 20 m apart. Player A runs
to the flagstaff. Before he reaches it, C makes a low pass to him. He
takes the ball along and dribbles in a slalom through the flagstaffs
and shoots at the goal. Player B sprints directly to the penalty area.
About 25 m in front of the goal, D makes a low pass at a right angle
to his running direction. Player B takes the ball along to the penalty
area boundary and shoots at the goal.

Objectives   1. Accurate passing into a teammate's running path.
2. Carrying the ball along quickly.
3. Effective dribbling while watching player B.
4. Making a low goal shot while running.

Comments   Player A should vary the speed at which he dribbles the ball so that
he does not shoot at the goal at the same time as player B.
The player shoots the ball, retrieves it and gives it to player C or D
and runs to the end of his group.

Ex. 126

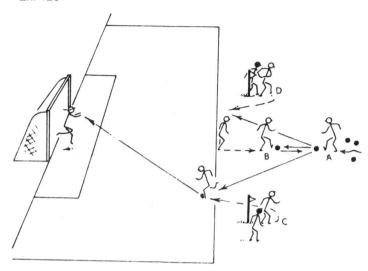

126

Participants A = 1 FP B = 1 FP C = 2 - 4 FP
               D = 2 - 4 FP   1 GK

Equipment   1 ball for each player of groups C and D
            2 flagstaffs

Description Set up the flagstaffs in the inside right and inside left positions about
20 m from the goal. Groups C and D take up positions here. Player
A dribbles the ball a few steps and makes a strong pass to player
B, who is running toward him. He deflects the ball gently. At the
same moment C sprints around the flagstaff toward the goal. Player
A immediately passes into C's running path. C shoots directly at the
goal. A's next pass is to D.

Objectives 1. Making a strong pass to a player.
2. Deflecting the ball gently.
3. Getting ready to receive a pass at the right moment.
4. Making a covered pass with the outer instep into a teammate's
running path.
5. Making a goal shot while running full speed.
6. Following up the goal shot.

Comment Do not attempt this exercise with less than six players; it will not
prove intensive for players A and B. The player who shoots at the
goal, sprints to fetch the ball, gives it to A, and runs back to his
group.

Ex. 127

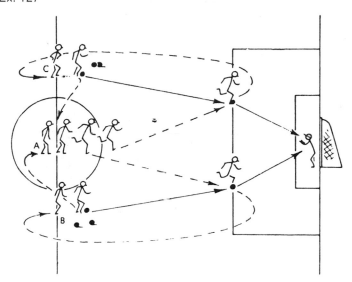

127

Participants   A = 2 - 8 FP   B = 1 FP   C = 1 FP   1 GK

Equipment   1 ball for each player of group A

Description   The first player of group A sprints to the inside left position. He receives an accurate, long pass in his running path from player C, shoots directly at the goal and runs around to group C. Player C changes to group A. The next player of group A sprints to the inside right position, receives a pass in his running path from player B, shoots directly at the goal, and runs around to group B. Player B also changes to group A. The next player runs to the inside left position again.

Objectives   1. Making an accurate, strong pass into a teammate's running path.
2. Making a direct goal shot while running full speed.
3. Building endurance.

Comments   If the emphasis is on endurance, no more than six players should participate. Two players alternate as ball fetchers.

Ex. 128

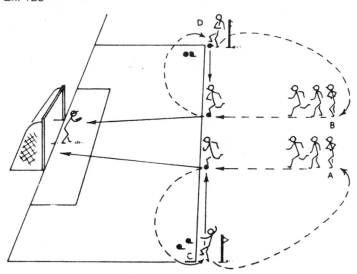

128

Participants A = 1 - 5 FP B = 1 - 5 FP C = 2 FP
                 D = 2 FP   1 GK

Equipment   1 ball for each player of groups A and B

Description The players of groups A and B sprint forward. Near the penalty area they receive strong, low passes at a right angle to their running directions from players C and D. The direct goal shot follows. After they pass, players C and D go the end of groups A and B, while players A and B run to C's and D's positions after the goal shot so that they may pass into the running paths of the next players in positions A and B.

Objectives   1. Making an accurate. low pass into a player's running path.
              2. Making a direct goal shot while running full speed.
              3. Building endurance.

Comments   If the third point is emphasized. then groups A and B should have only 2 players. Two players alternate fetching the ball.

Ex. 129

Ex. 130

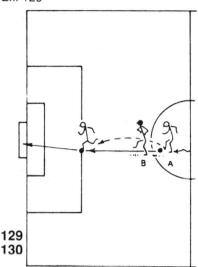

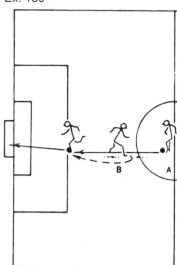

129
130

Participants   A = 1 - 8 FP   B = 1 FP

Equipment   1 ball for each player

Description   **Exercise 129:** Player B stands with wide straddled legs about 25 m from the goal. Player A dribbles the ball to B, makes a strong pass through B's legs, sprints immediately after the ball and shoots it at the goal from the penalty area boundary.

Exercise 130: Player B stands about 25 m from the goal with wide-straddled legs facing A, who is 3 m away from him. Player A makes a low, strong pass through B's straddled legs from a standing position. B turns immediately, sprints after the ball and tries to reach it before entering the penalty area. The ball is shot at the goal while running full speed.

Objectives   1. Improving acceleration speed.
2. Improving running speed.
3. Following up the goal shot.

Comments   The distances can vary. Since speed is the main point, less attention is paid to the execution of the goal shot. A GK is not essential. If there are many players in Exercise 129, B is replaced only after all players of group A have shot at the goal. In Exercise 130, A makes the passes until the CO calls for a change. If there are a large number of players, they can practise in two sections alongside each other.

Ex. 131

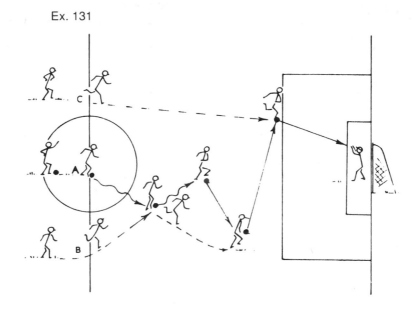

131

Participants 3 - 9 FP 1 GK

Equipment 1 ball for every 3 players

Description Player A dribbles the ball toward the inside right position. B immediately leaves his position and cuts off A's path, taking over the ball. After dribbling the ball briefly, however, he passes the ball back to A, who has reached the inside right position by now. In the meantime, C is ready to receive a pass in the inside left position. A immediately makes a diagonal pass to C, who shoots directly at the goal.

Objectives 1. Taking over the ball from a teammate.
2. Making accurate, covered passes.
3. Making an accurate, wide pass into a teammate's running path.
4. Making a direct, low, strong goal shot.
5. Following up the goal shot.

Comments For these or similar actions to succeed in a match, they must be practised frequently. It is recommended that the same pair of players practise together so that they get used to playing together. The player who shoots at the goal sprints to fetch the ball and dribbles it at a moderate running pace to player A's starting position. Player A has changed to group C in the meantime.

Ex. 132

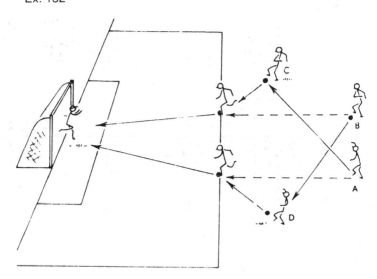

132

Participants A = 2 - 5 FP   B = 2 - 5 FP   C = 1 FP
              D = 1 FP   1 GK

Equipment   1 ball for each player of groups A and B

Description The first player of groups A and B each passes his ball diagonally
             to players C and D almost at the same time. Immediately after the
             pass, A and B sprint forward. Players D and C deflect the passes:
             player D's ball into A's running path, player C into B's. Both shoot
             directly at the goal.

Objectives   1. Making accurate, strong passes with the outer instep.
             2. Passing and sprinting.
             3. Letting the strongly passed ball rebound gently.
             4. Shooting directly on goal while running full speed.

Comments   Players C and D are replaced after a certain time. No more than six
             players should practise at one time. After a successful goal shot,
             players A and B immediately retrieve their balls, leave the playing
             zone, and return to their starting positions.

Ex. 133

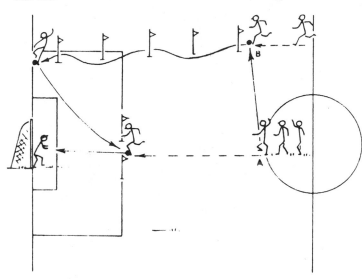

133

Participants 2 - 10 FP   1 GK

Equipment   1 ball for every two players
             7 flagstaffs

Description Player A makes a low pass to B, who immediately moves the ball
             forward and runs in slalom through the flagstaffs that have been set
             up. Player A watches B's slalom run and sprints forward only when
             he believes he will be able to reach the ball centre-passed by B
             while it is still in the air. He shoots directly at the goal.

Objectives   1. Making accurate, low passes.
             2. Dribbling the ball in slalom and with varying speed.
             3. Making an accurate centre pass into a running path.
             4. Running toward the ball at the right moment.
             5. Making a direct goal shot.

Comments   This exercise is good for less experienced players. Pay special
             attention to dribbling the ball at varying speeds and to running
             toward the ball at the right moment.
             The distance between the flagstaffs should be from 3 to 8 m.

Ex. 134

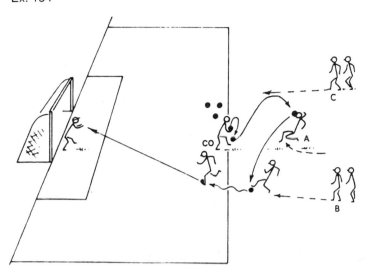

134

Participants   A = 1 FP   B = 2 - 4 FP   C = 2 - 4 FP   1 GK

Equipment   1 ball for every player in groups B and C

Description   The CO passes high to player A. He heads directly to the player of group B who is ready to receive the header. B moves the ball forward briefly and shoots at the goal. The next header goes to a player of group C who is in the open.

Objectives   1. Heading the ball into a teammate's running path.
2. Getting into the open at the right moment.
3. Moving the ball forward quickly.
4. Making the goal shot while running full speed.
5. Following up the goal shot.

Comments   To exercise player A to the fullest extent, groups B and C should have at least 2 players. To train player A's reaction ability, the players of groups B and C should not alternate getting ready to receive passes. The player who shoots at the goal sprints to fetch the ball, gives it to the CO and runs to the end of his group.

Ex. 135

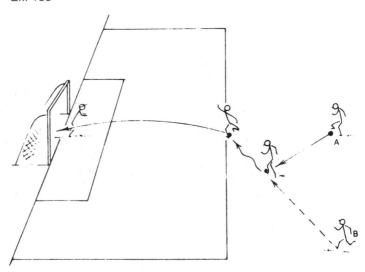

135

Participants   A = 1 FP   B = 1 - 9 FP   1 GK

Equipment   1 ball for every player of group B

Description   Player A makes a low pass into the running path of B, who is sprinting diagonally across the playing field. Player B dribbles the ball a few steps and makes a strong shot at the goal from the penalty area boundary.

Objectives   1. Making accurate, low passes into the running path of a player.
2. Moving the ball forward quickly.
3. Making a strong, low goal shot from a turn.
4. Following up the goal shot.

Comments   With advanced players, the CO can begin this exercise with a pass to player A. The pass must be made so that A has to turn to carry the ball forward. Now B watches for the right moment to receive a pass.
Each player sprints to fetch the ball shot at the goal, gives it to A. and runs to the end of his group.

Ex. 136

136

Participants   2 - 10 FP   1 GK

Equipment   1 ball for every two players

Description   Player A makes a low pass to B, who is running toward him, and sprints toward the goal. Player B fakes a direct pass and carries the ball in the opposite direction. In the meantime, player A has stopped sprinting; but as soon as B looks for someone to pass to, A sprints forward again. B passes immediately into A's running path. While A runs farther toward the goal with the ball, B has started sprinting forward immediately after the pass. At the right moment A passes back to B who shoots directly at the goal.

Objectives   1. Moving the ball in the opposite direction after faking a direct pass.
2. Passing and sprinting.
3. Getting into the open to receive a pass.
4. Making an accurate, low pass into a teammate's running path.
5. Making a back pass while running full speed.
6. Making a positioned goal shot.
7. Correct rhythm change in individual moves.

Comments   Only frequent practice will achieve the desired precision. It is useful if players are partnered, for example, IL and OL, or OL and LH.

Ex. 137

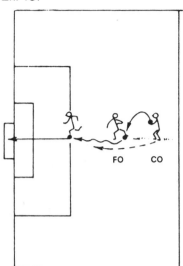

FO   CO

Ex. 138

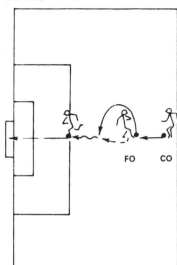

FO   CO

137
138

Participants   1 - 5 FP   1 GK

Equipment   1 ball for each player

Description   **Exercise 137:** The CO throws or shoots the ball high to a player standing 20 m in front of the goal. The player carries the ball forward and shoots at the goal from the penalty area boundary.

Exercise 138: The CO makes a strong, low pass to the player. After taking the ball along quickly, he shoots the ball at the goal from the penalty area boundary.

Objectives   1. Moving the ball forward quickly and keeping it low.
2. Carrying the ball in combination moves (controlling and carrying it along).
3. Making a strong, low goal shot while running full speed.
4. Following up the goal shot.

Comments   Several players may play at the same time. Each player sprints to fetch the ball he has shot at the goal and goes outside of the shooting zone back to his starting position. To be able to cut off the ball correctly in Exercise 138, a perfectly level playing surface is necessary, at least in the space between the CO and the player.

Ex. 139

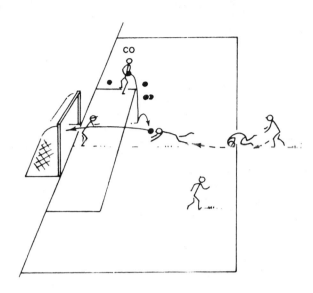

139

Participants 1 - 5 FP   1 GK

Equipment   1 ball for every player

Description: The FP stand in a row on the penalty area boundary. The first player
runs a few steps, then does a forward roll. As soon as he starts to
get up, the CO throws him a ball from the corner of the goal area.
He dives to head it into the goal.

Objectives   1. Training agility.
2. Training reaction capability.
3. Correct heading from a dive.
4. Following up the header.

Comments   The players are to stand up quickly after the header, sprint to fetch
the ball, give it to the CO, and run back to their starting positions.

Ex. 140

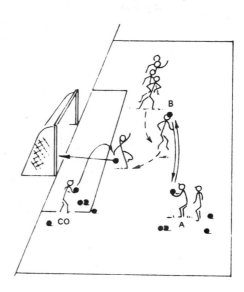

140

Participants   A = 2 - 5 FP   B = 2 - 5 FP   1 GK

Equipment   1 ball for each player

Description   The first player of group B runs toward A. The first player of this group throws a ball high to him. Player B immediately heads the ball back and turns quickly toward the goal. Now the CO throws or kicks a ball to him so that he can shoot directly at goal from the air. Both players change positions.

Objectives   1. Making a header pass from a jump.
2. Passing and sprinting.
3. Making a goal shot from the air.
4. Following up the goal shot.
5. Building concentration.

Comments   The player immediately sprints to fetch the ball shot at the goal, brings it back to the CO, then runs to the end of group A.

Ex. 141

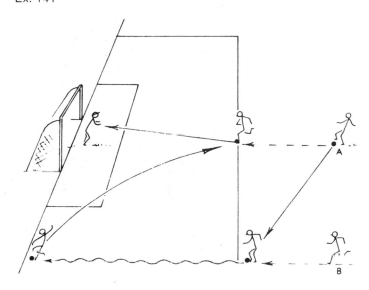

141

Participants   2 to 10 FP   1 GK

Equipment   1 ball for every two players

Description Player A makes a strong, low pass into the running path of player B who is sprinting forward. Player B moves the ball forward quickly, and just before the baseline makes a centre pass to the foot of player A who has run farther and who shoots directly at the goal.

Objectives   1. Making a covered pass with the outer instep.
             2. Carrying the ball forward quickly.
             3. Fast dribbling.
             4. Accurate centre pass.
             5. Making a direct goal shot from the air.
             6. Following up the goal shot.

Comments   The exercise can be made easier for less experienced players. Player B runs to the penalty area line and centre-passes from there. Player A controls the ball briefly first before shooting at the goal. The player who shoots at the goal sprints to fetch the ball and dribbles it while running back to the starting position.

Ex. 142

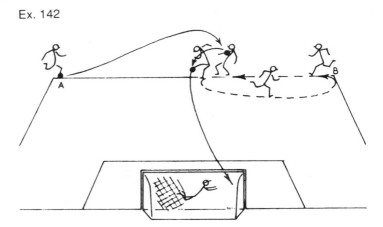

142

Participants   A = 1 FP   B = 1 - 5 FP   1 GK

Equipment   1 ball for each player of group B

Description   Player A makes a half-high centre pass from the corner of the penalty area to player B. The pass must be calculated in such a way that player B, who is in the open, controls the ball with his chest and shoots at the goal as soon as possible.

Objectives   1. Making an accurate, half-high pass into a teammate's running path.
2. Controlling the ball with the chest.
3. Making a goal shot from the air.
4. Following up the goal shot.

Comments   To master the half-high pass. the centre pass is made alternately with the inner and outer instep kick. In addition, the player of group B should run at different speeds.
Each player of group B sprints to fetch the ball he has shot at the goal. passes it to A and runs to the end of his group. Player A is replaced only after his concentration begins to fade.

Ex. 143

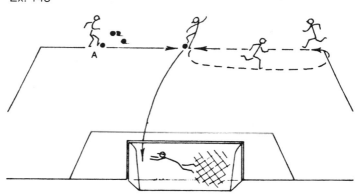

143

Participants   A = 1 FP   B = 1 - 5 FP   1 GK

Equipment   1 ball for each player of group B

Description   Player A makes a low pass from the corner of the penalty area along
               the penalty area line to the player of group B running toward him.
               B turns and shoots the ball directly at the goal.

Objectives   1. Making the well-aimed low pass.
               2. Running toward the ball.
               3. Making the direct goal shot from a turn.
               4. Following up the goal shot.

Comments   Each player immediately sprints to retrieve the ball he has shot at
              the goal, passes it to A and runs to the end of his group.
              Player A may be replaced after a certain time.

Ex. 144

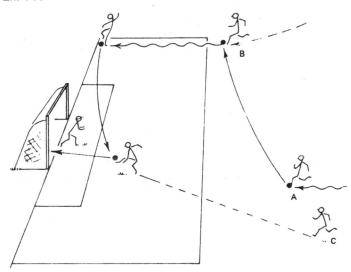

144

Participants   3 - 9 FP   1 GK

Equipment   1 ball for every three players

Description   Player B sprints forward. A immediately centre-passes into B's running path. B dribbles the ball on the edge of the baseline and centre-passes it to the foot of C, who has also run forward and who now shoots directly at the goal.

Objectives   1. Making the wide, diagonal pass into a teammate's running path.
2. Timing in receiving the pass.
3. Accurate centre-passing.
4. Making a direct goal shot.
5. Following up the goal shot.

Comments   The playing and shooting zone must be cleared immediately. Player C sprints after the ball shot at the goal and dribbles it quickly to group A.
In the meantime, player A has moved to group C.

Ex. 145

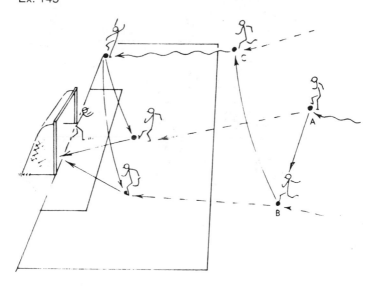

145

Participants 3 - 9 FP   1 GK
Equipment   1 ball for every three players

Description   After dribbling briefly to the inside right position, A passes the ball
              into the running path of B, who is ready to receive the pass. He
              makes a direct wide centre pass into C's running path on the other
              side of the playing field. C dribbles until he approaches the baseline
              and centre-passes alternately to A's or B's foot. The ball is shot
              directly at the goal by either.

Objectives   1. Making an accurate, covered pass into a teammate's running
              path.
              2. Making a correct diagonal pass.
              3. Fast dribbling.
              4. Accurate centre-passing.
              5. Making a direct goal shot.

Comments   The playing and shooting zone must be cleared immediately. The
              player who has shot at the goal, retrieves the ball immediately and
              dribbles it quickly to group A. The player should not be watching the
              ball alone when dribbling. The head should be kept high.

Ex. 146

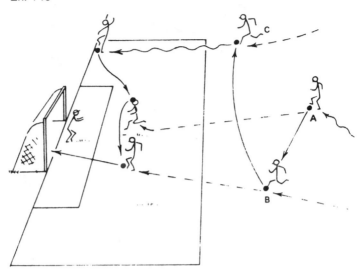

146

Participants 3 - 12 FP   1 GK

Equipment   1 ball for every 3 players

Description After dribbling the ball briefly to the inside right position, A passes
the ball into the running path of B, who is presenting himself. B
makes a direct, wide, centre pass into C's running path on the other
side of the field. C dribbles the ball until near the baseline and
centre-passes to the penalty mark. Player A heads the ball to B,
who makes a positioned shot at the goal.

Objectives   1. Making an accurate covered pass into a player's running path.
2. Teaching the diagonal pass.
3. Fast dribbling.
4. Accurate centre-passing.
5. Correct heading.
6. Making a precise goal shot.
7. Following up the goal shot.

Comments   The playing and shooting zone must be cleared immediately. The
player who has shot at the goal sprints to retrieve the ball and gives
it to A.

Ex. 147

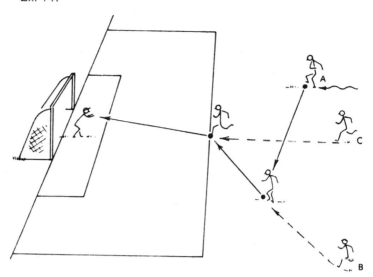

147

Participants   3 - 12 FP   1 GK

Equipment   1 ball for every three players

Description: Player A dribbles the ball a few steps. In a burst of speed, B sprints
              into the open. A immediately makes a strong, low pass into his
              running path. Before the ball reaches B, C sprints forward. Player
              B deflects the ball into C's running path. C shoots at the goal.

Objectives   1. Getting into the open at the right moment.
             2. Making a strong, low pass.
             3. Deflecting the ball gently into a teammate's running path.
             4. Making the strong, low goal shot.
             5. Following up the goal shot.

Comments   The player who shoots at the goal, sprints to retrieve the ball and
             goes to position A. Player A changes to B, who changes to C.

Ex. 148

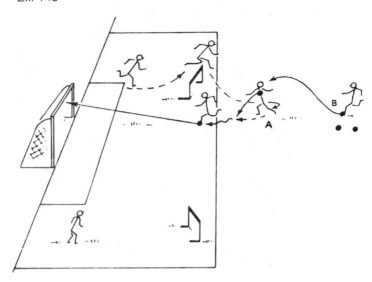

148

Participants   A = 1 - 5 FP   B = 1 FP   1 GK

Equipment   1 ball for each player of group A
1 hurdle

Description   Player B stands about 40 m away from the goal; player A about 20 m away. Player B centre-passes the ball to A's chest. A carries the ball along quickly and shoots at the goal from the penalty area boundary. After the goal shot, A jumps over the hurdle, and returns to his starting position.

Objectives   1. Making an accurate, half-high pass.
2. Moving the ball forward quickly with the chest.
3. Making an aimed goal shot.
4. Building endurance.
5. Training jumping ability.

Comments   If objective 4 is to be stressed, no more than two players should practise at the same time. In addition, several balls should be available to avoid interruptions during the exercise.

Ex. 149

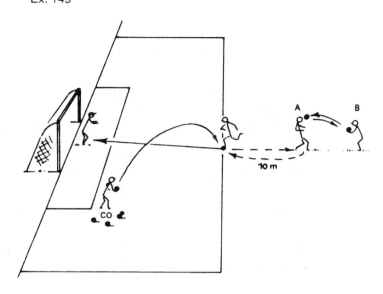

149

Participants   A = 1 - 5 FP   B = 1 FP   1GK

Equipment   1 ball for each player of group A

Description   Player B throws the ball high to player A, who is standing 5 m away, so that A must jump to head it back. Player A turns around immediately after the jump and sprints to the penalty area. Now the CO throws a ball high to him. A shoots the ball at the goal directly with a drop kick, or after carrying the ball along briefly.

Objectives   1. Making the fast turn after the jump.
2. Making the strong goal shot while running full speed.
3. Following up the goal shot.
4. Teaching concentration.

Comments   Player B is replaced after significant practice. The player who shoots at the goal sprints to retrieve the ball, gives it to the CO, and sits down at the end of group A.

Ex. 150

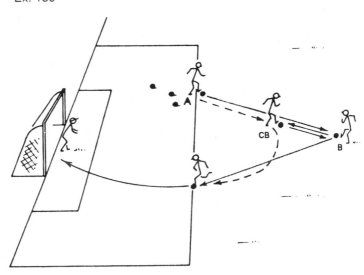

150

Participants   A = 1 - 5 FP   B = 1 FP   1 GK

Equipment   1 ball for every two players

Description   Player A makes a low pass to B from the penalty area boundary and
               runs toward him immediately. Player B deflects the ball back to A.
               A passes directly back again, but less powerfully. After the pass he
               turns and sprints to the penalty area. Player B passes the ball,
               without stopping it, into A's running path. A shoots from the penalty
               area boundary.

Objectives   1. Making an accurate, strong pass into a teammate's running path.
               2. Passing and sprinting.
               3. Deflecting the ball gently.
               4. Making an aimed goal shot with a spin.
               5. Following up the goal shot.

Comments   The direct pass succeeds only if the playing surface is level.
               Player B is replaced after a thorough practice. Player A follows up
               by sprinting to retrieve the the ball shot at the goal and dribbles back
               to the starting position.

Ex. 151

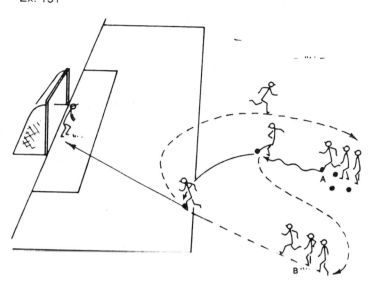

151

Participants 2 - 10 FP 1 GK

Equipment 1 ball for every two players

Description While A is slowly dribbling the ball, B sprints forward. A immediately passes into B's running path and B shoots directly at the goal. Afterwards both players change positions.

Objectives 1. Making the covered pass with the outer instep.
2. Making the low goal shot while running full speed.
3. Following up the goal shot.

Comments Player A must pass accurately so that the ball quickly reaches player B. The player who shoots at the goal retrieves it first and then goes outside of the playing and shooting zone to the end of group A.

Ex. 152

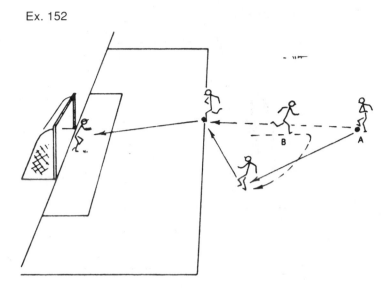

152

Participants   2 - 10 FP   1 GK

Equipment   1 ball for every two players

Description   Player A dribbles the ball and B runs slowly towards him. A passes immediately into B's running path and then sprints forward so that, after reaching the ball, B can pass the ball directly into A's running path. A shoots at the goal.

Objectives   1. Making the covered pass with the outer instep into the a teammate's running path.
2. Passing and immediately sprinting.
3. Accurate passing at a right angle to the running direction while running full speed.
4. Making direct, strong, low goal shots.
5. Following up the goal shot.

Comments   Players A and B change places after every completed play. The player who has made the goal shot sprints to retrieve the ball and dribbles it at a moderate running speed to the starting position of group A.

Ex. 153

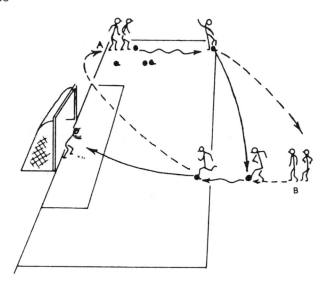

153

Participants   2 - 10 FP   1 GK

Equipment   1 ball for each player

Description   Player A dribbles the ball along the penalty area line. Player B is
ready to receive a pass and sprints forward before player A has left
the penalty area. He centre passes the ball with his left foot into B's
running path. B carries the ball forward briefly and shoots at the
goal.

Objectives   1. Getting into the open at the right moment.
2. Making an accurate centre pass into the teammate's running
path.
3. Carrying the ball along quickly.
4. Making a positioned goal shot with a spin.
5. Immediately running on after the pass or goal shot.

Comments   The player who makes the goal shot first sprints to retrieve the ball
and then goes to group A. If only a small number of players are
participating and there are enough balls, this exercise can be used
effectively to build endurance. The players continue practising until
the CO calls for a stop.

Ex. 154

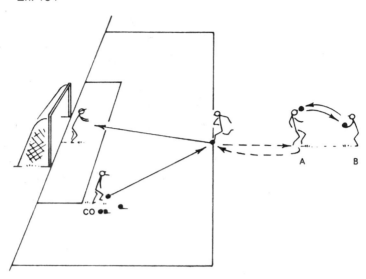

154

Participants   A = 1 - 5 FP   B = 1 FP   1 GK

Equipment   1 ball for each player of group A

Description   Player B throws the ball high to player A who is 5 m away, so that A must jump to head it. Player A turns immediately after the jump and sprints to the penalty area. Now the CO makes a low pass to him, which he shoots directly at the goal.

Objectives   1. Fast turning after a jump.
2. Making a strong goal shot while running full speed.
3. Following up the goal shot.
4. Building concentration.

Comments   Less experienced players may control the ball first after the low pass and then shoot at the goal. Player B may be replaced after a certain time. The player who shoots at the goal first sprints to retrieve the ball, gives it to the CO, and sits down at the end of group A.

Ex. 155

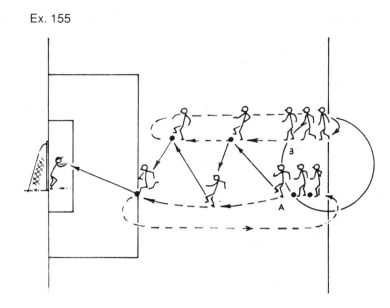

155

Participants   2 - 10 FP   1 GK

Equipment   1 ball for every two players

Description   Players A and B make strong, low passes to each other in a zig-zag
pattern. The ball is shot at the goal from the penalty area boundary.
The players run over the field sides at a moderate tempo back to
their starting positions.

Objectives   1. Making a strong, low, accurate pass into a teammate's running
path.
2. Making a direct pass.
3. Making a strong, low goal shot from a full-speed run.
4. Following up the goal shot.

Comments   The player who shoots at the goal, immediately retrieves the ball
and goes to the end of the group. Make sure that the passes reach
the partner quickly. Advanced players should practise at a fast
running pace.

Ex. 156

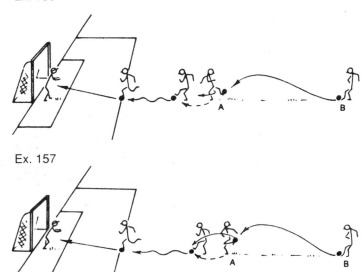

Ex. 157

156
157

Participants   A = 1 - 5 FP   B = 1 FP   1 GK

Equipment   1 ball for every player of group A

Description   **Exercise 156:** Player B stands 40 m in front of the goal and passes the ball half high to player A, standing 20 m away. A carries the ball along from the air, while turning. After dribbling the ball briefly, he shoots at the goal from the penalty area boundary while running full speed.

Exercise 157: Set up and passing sequence as in exercise 156. But player A carries the ball to the goal with the outside of the foot, and shoots at the goal after dribbling briefly.

Objectives   1. Making an accurate, half-high pass.
2. Moving the ball quickly from a starting position facing the goal.
3. Making a low, strong goal shot while running full speed.
4. Following up the goal shot.

Comments   Player B is replaced after a certain number of passes. Advanced players shoot at the goal after carrying the ball forward, without dribbling first.
The player who shoots at the goal, sprints to retrieve the ball, passes it to B and goes to the end of group A.

Ex. 158

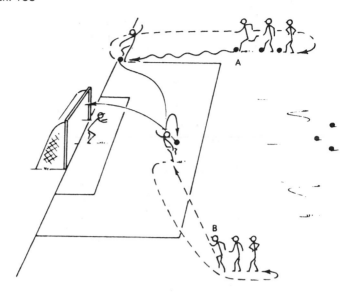

158

Participants   2 - 8 FP   1 GK

Equipment   1 ball for every two players

Description   Player A dribbles the ball along the right boundary of the penalty area and centre passes to the penalty mark from the baseline. Player B runs to the penalty mark only after A has passed. He shoots the ball, which has bounced once, directly at the goal from the air. Both players go to the end of their groups.

Objectives   1. Fast Dribbling.
2. Accurate centre-passing to the penalty mark.
3. Direct shot from the air and from a turn.
4. Following up the goal shot.

Comments   The player who shoots at the goal, sprints to retrieve the ball and passes it to group A. Make sure that the ball is not shot from the air with maximum power, but is a positioned shot.

Ex. 159

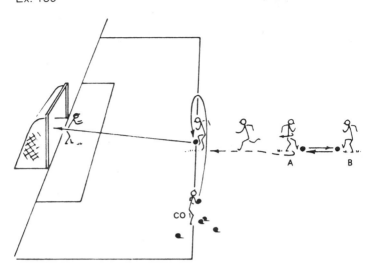

159

Participants   A = 1 - 5 FP   B = 1 FP   1 GK

Equipment   1 ball for every player of group A

Description   Player B makes a low, strong pass to A, who immediately deflects the ball, turns quickly and sprints toward the goal. On the penalty area boundary, the CO throws a high ball to A who shoots at the goal either directly from the air or after carrying the ball forward.

Objectives   1. Deflecting the ball gently.
2. Quick turning.
3. Taking along briefly a ball coming high from the side.
4. Making a strong, low goal shot from a full run.
5. Following up the goal shot.

Comments   Player B remains passer until the CO replaces him. The CO can vary the passes. e.g. 1) low. 2) with a bounce. 3) centre pass from the penalty area boundary. The player who shoots at the goal, sprints to retrieve the ball, gives it to the CO, and runs to the end of the group.

Ex. 160

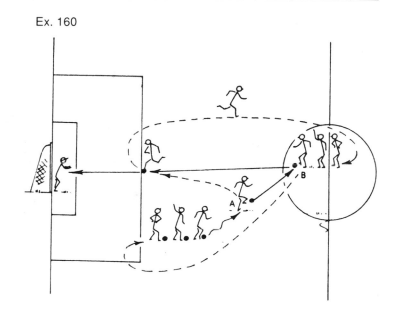

160

Participants 2 -10 FP   1GK

Equipment   1 ball for every two players

Description Player A dribbles the ball a few metres toward B, makes a strong
pass to him and sprints toward the goal. Player B receives the ball
and makes a covered pass into A's running path. A shoots directly
at the goal.

Objectives   1. Making a strong, low pass to a player.
2. Making a covered pass with the outer instep into a teammate's
running path.
3. Passing and sprinting.
4. Making a strong, low goal shot while running full speed.
5. Following up the goal shot.

Comments   As the players of group A immediately follow-up by sprinting to
retrieve the ball and move to the end of group B; the players of group
B sprint a few steps after the pass and then run slowly to the end
of group A.

Ex. 161

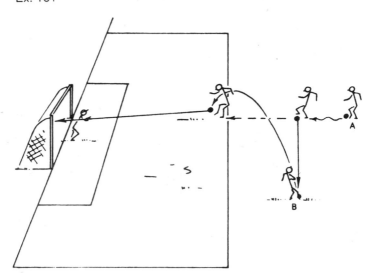

161

Participants A = 1 - 6 FP   B = 1 FP   1 GK

Equipment 1 ball for each player of group A

Description Player A dribbles the ball. When he is almost at the same level as B, he passes accurately to him and at the same time sprints forward. Player B passes the strong, low spinning ball high into A's running path. He takes the ball along briefly or shoots directly at the goal.

Objectives 1. Practising the wall pass.
2. Carrying briefly a high-spinning ball.

Comments Not all the technical and tactical game moves for the wall pass described on page 10 of this book are relevant here. Player B does not let the ball rebound, but makes a direct, high pass with a spin. In a match, this type of pass is often required, especially when free spaces are very small. Because this kick is very difficult, it should only be done only by advanced players.

Ex. 162

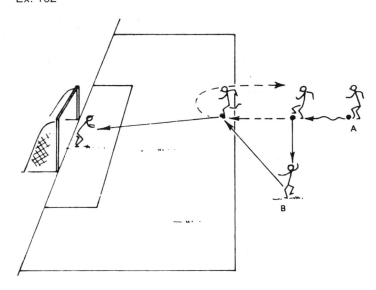

162

Participants   A = 1 - 6 FP   B = 1 FP   1 GK

Equipment   1 ball for every two players

Description   Player A dribbles the ball until B is almost at the same level. He then passes accurately to B and at the same time sprints forward. Player B deflects the strongly passed ball into the running path of A, who shoots directly at the goal.

Objectives   1. Teaching the wall pass.
              2. Making a strong, low pass while running full speed.
              3. Following up the goal shot.

Comments   So that deflecting the ball may be mastered, the player is replaced only after considerable practice. After a successful goal shot, the player sprints to retrieve the ball and dribbles it outside of the shooting zone, back to the end of group A. Pay strict attention to the description of the wall pass on page 10.

Ex. 163

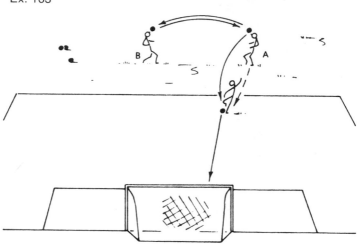

163

Participants A = 1 - 5 FP   B = 1 FP   1 GK

Equipment   1 ball for each player

Description   Players A and B stand 20 m from the goal, 5 m apart. They head the
              ball a few times to each other until A lays the ball on to the goal with
              his head. sprints forward and shoots at the goal while running full
              speed.

Objectives   1. Accurate heading.
              2. Proper laying on of the ball.
              3. Making a positioned goal shot.
              4. Following up the goal shot.

Comments   Player B remains the passer until the CO replaces him. If the ball
              which has been laid on. bounces so unfavourably that it cannot be
              shot directly at the goal. it is carried along and then shot at the goal.
              The players of group A sprint to retrieve the ball shot at the goal and
              go outside of the playing area to the end of the group.

Ex. 164

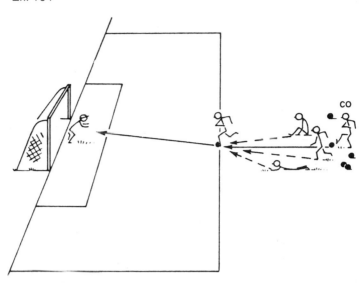

164

Participants   Up to 8 FP

Equipment   1 ball for each player

Description   The CO stands with the balls about 20 m from the penalty area
boundary. Just in front of him, a FP stands, sits or lies. The CO
makes a low pass to the player on his right or left. As soon as the
player sees the ball, he sprints after it and tries to reach it as quickly
as possible. He shoots at the goal while running full speed. While
the first player runs after his ball and dribbles it outside of the
shooting zone back to his group, the next player has already started
sprinting.

Objectives   1. Improving reaction ability.
2. Improving acceleration and running speed.
3. Making a low goal shot while running full speed.

Comments   If several players are available, this exercise may be carried out as
a competition. As may be seen in the diagram, players take various
positions and, of course, are different distances to the CO. The
player who reaches the ball first, may shoot at the goal.

Ex. 165

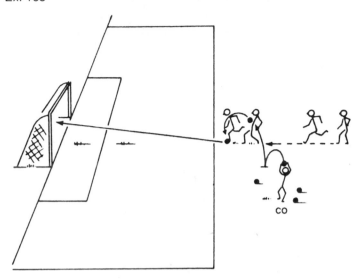

165

Participants   Up to 8 FP

Equipment   1 ball for every player

Description   The CO places the balls about 20 m from the baseline at the same level as the end of the goal area line. The players take position in front of the middle of the goal, about 40 m from the baseline. The first player sprints toward the penalty area. At the right moment the CO throws a ball with both hands onto the ground so that the player must move it along with his chest from a jump. After briefly laying the ball on, the player shoots at the goal. The player then sprints to the ball to retrieve it, dribbles it outside of the shooting zone to the CO, and quickly goes back to his starting position.

Objectives   1. Improving running speed.
2. Carrying the ball along briefly with the chest from a jump.
3. Making a low goal shot at full speed.
4. Following up the goal shot.

Comments   Through constant practice, the player can learn to move the ball forward with his chest well enough that the ball can be shot at the goal directly from the air. The whole move must take place quickly.

Ex. 166

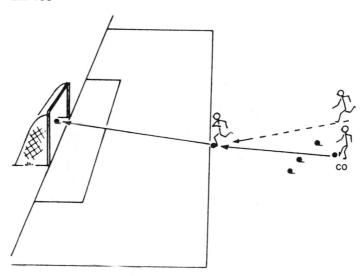

166

Participants   Up to 8 FP

Equipment   1 ball for each player

Description   The CO stands with the balls about 20 m from the penalty area boundary. A player stands beside him. As soon as the player sprints forward and is ready to receive a pass, the CO feeds the ball. The ball must be fed so that the player can shoot directly at the goal from the penalty area boundary while running full speed. While the first player runs after his ball and dribbles it outside of the shooting zone to his starting position, the next player is already sprinting.

Objectives   1. Improving running speed.
2. Making a low, goal shot while running full speed.

Comments   If there are several players, the CO lets one player pass. After a certain time, another player takes his place. Each player sprints to retrieve his ball and returns from the shooting area to his starting position.

Ex. 167

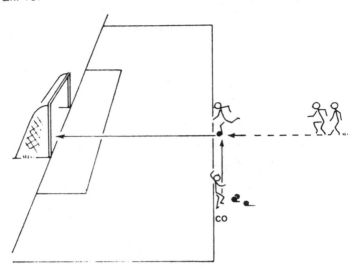

167

Participants Up to 8 FP

Equipment 1 ball for each player

Description: The CO stands with the balls on the penalty area boundary at the same level as the side line of the goal area. The players take position in front of the middle of the goal, about 20 m from the penalty area. The first player sprints toward the penalty area. The CO passes the ball into his running path and he shoots directly at the goal. After the goal shot, the player sprints after the ball, retrieves it, dribbles it outside of the shooting zone to the CO and goes back to the starting position.

Objectives 1. Improving running speed.
2. Making a direct, low goal shot while running full speed.
3. Following up the goal shot.

Comments Less experienced players do not shoot directly at the goal. The ball is briefly carried forward briefly and shot.
If there is no GK, the goal is divided into three parts with two jumping ropes. The CO calls out the corner of the goal at which the ball must be shot just before the goal shot is made.

Ex. 168

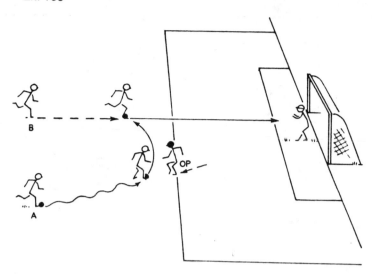

168

Participants   2 FP = one group   1 OP

Equipment   1 ball for each group

Description   Players A and B of one group take position about 25 m away from the goal. The OP is standing on the penalty area boundary.
Player A dribbles the ball toward his opponent. As soon as the OP attacks, A passes to B who is running into the opening. B either shoots directly at the goal or shoots after briefly carrying the ball forward. The next group immediately moves toward the opponent.

Objectives   1. Observing the opponent while dribbling the ball.
2. Running into the open.
3. Making the covered pass.
4. Making the direct, low goal shot.

Comments   To make this exercise as realistic as possible, let A decide if he wants to dribble around the OP or pass the ball to his partner. Player A must react properly to the OP's actions.
The player who shoots at the goal, sprints to retrieve the ball and goes back to the starting position.

Ex. 169

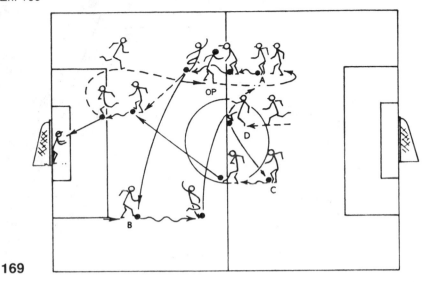

169

Participants A = 1 - 5 FP   B = 2 FP   C = 2 FP
D = 1 FP   1 OP   1 GK

Equipment   6 balls

Description   The first player of group A dribbles the ball toward the OP, dribbles around him and immediately centre passes to B. During this, player A runs along the wing into the penalty area. Player C makes a low pass to him. A shoots at the goal after briefly carrying the ball forward. Player B controls the ball passed to him, centre passes to player D, and runs back to his starting position. Player D passes all the balls back to C or A.

Objectives   1. Dribbling.
2. Teaching the diagonal pass.
3. Passing and sprinting.
4. Accurate passing into a teammate's running path.
5. Carrying the ball forward quickly.
6. Following up the goal shot.

Comments   Player A sprints to retrieve the ball shot at the goal and slowly runs outside of the playing zone to the end of group A. Good conditions (good playing surface, good balls, and no disturbing wind) are necessary for a smooth exercise. At first the OP only attacks passively. Players B, C, and D trade places after a certain time.

Ex. 170

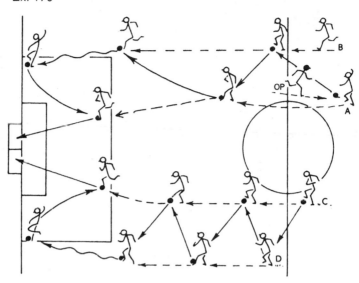

170

Participants   8 - 16 FP   1 OP   1 GK

Equipment   1 ball for every two players

Description   The attack is carried out in two different sections.

> **Section I:** Shortly before A is tackled by the OP, B runs into the open. Player A immediately makes a covered pass to B and sprints forward. He deflects the ball gently into A's running path and sprints forward. A immediately passes into B's running path. B carries the ball along to the baseline and centre passes to the foot of A, who is in the open and who shoots at the goal directly from the air.

> **Section II:** The ball is passed in a zig-zag pattern until D carries the ball along to the baseline and centre passes to the foot of C, who is in the open. C shoots directly at the goal from the air.

Objectives   1. Accurately passing into a teammate's running path.
              2. Deflecting the ball gently.
              3. Accurate centre passing.
              4. Making a direct goal shot from the air.

Comments   Practising in two sections is effective only when many players are present and an intensive level of exercise is achieved.

Ex. 171

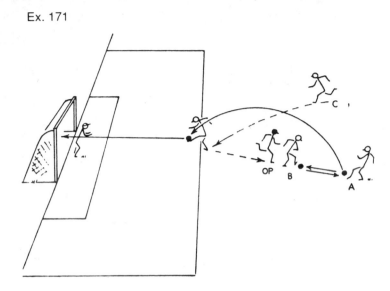

171

Participants   A = 1 FP   B = 1 FP   C = 1 - 5 FP   1 OP   1 GK

Equipment   1 ball for each player of group C

Description   Player A passes to B who is in the open. Since he is being followed closely by the OP, he deflects the ball to A. A player of group C immediately sprints forward and receives a direct, half-high pass from A in his running path. Player C shoots directly at the goal while running full speed.

Objectives   1. Running into the right moment.
              2. Accurate passing to another player.
              3. Deflecting the ball gently.
              4. Making a direct half-high pass into a teammate's running path.
              5. Making a goal shot while running full speed.
              6. Following up the goal shot.

Comments   Players of groups A and B stay in these positions for a short period of time. Each player of group C sprints to retrieve the ball shot at the goal, dribbles it slowly to A and goes to the end of his group.

Ex. 172

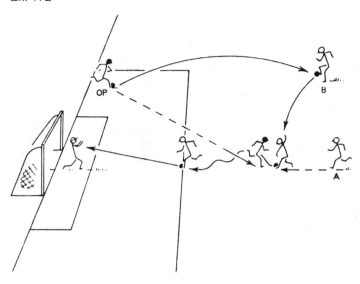

172

Participants   A = 1 - 5 FP   B = 1 FP   1 - 3 OP   1 GK

Equipment   1 ball for each OP

Description   The OP makes a high centre pass to B from the goal line. B passes
               the ball from the air to A, who is in the open. Player A carries the ball
               along to the goal, dribbles around the OP, who has sprinted forward
               after passing, and shoots at the goal from the penalty circle.

Objectives   1. Accurate, high passing.
               2. Getting into the open at the right moment.
               3. Passing the ball directly into a teammate's running path.
               4. Correct dribbling.
               5. Making a low goal shot after dribbling the ball quickly.

Comments   All OP go quickly back to their starting positions. Player A sprints to
               retrieve the ball shot at the goal, gives it to the OP and runs to his
               starting position. Player B trades positions with OP.

Ex. 173

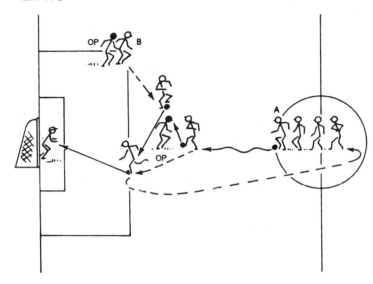

173

Participants A = 1 to 5 FP B = 1 FP 2 OP 1 GK

Equipment 1 ball for each player of group A

Description: The setup can be seen in the diagram. The first player of group A dribbles the ball toward the OP. Shortly before A is attacked by the OP, B gets free from his OP and runs into the open. Player A makes a covered pass to B and sprints forward. Player B lets the ball rebound gently into A's running path. Player A shoots directly at the goal. Player B and both OP immediately return to their starting positions, and the second player of group A runs with the ball toward the OP.

Objectives 1. Fast dribbling.
2. Practising the wall pass.
3. Making a direct goal shot while running full speed.
4. Getting free from the OP and running into the open.
5. Following up the goal shot.

Comments The players sprint to retrieve the ball shot at the goal and go quickly to the end of the group. Player B is replaced after a certain number of passes. After the exercise has been mastered, let player A decide if he wishes to use the wall pass or to outplay the OP with a passing feint.
Pay close attention to the wall pass move described on page 10.

Ex. 174

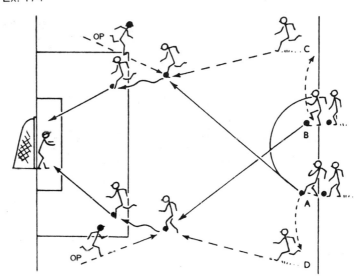

174

Participants 6 - 10 FP   2 OP   1 GK

Equipment   1 ball for each player of group A and B

Description   The players of groups A and B take position each with his ball in the central circle. Players C and D stand to the side, about 10 m from the goal. The OP stand at the corners of the penalty area. Player C sprints toward the goal. Player A passes the ball into C's running path so that the OP on this side cannot interrupt the ball. Player C outruns OP and, after dribbling the ball briefly, shoots it at the goal. Before C shoots at the goal, D sprints toward the goal. B immediately passes the ball into his running path so that the OP on that side cannot interrupt it. The OP is again outrun, and the ball, after being dribbled, is shot at the goal. After the pass, players A and B go immediately to position C or D at the side.

Objectives   1. Accurate, strong passing into a teammate's running path.
2. Carrying the ball along quickly.
3. Correctly outrunning the OP.
4. Making a goal shot while running full speed.
5. Following up the goal shot.

Comments   The player who shoots at the goal, sprints to retrieve the ball and passes it back to group A or B. The OP must quickly return to their starting positions.

Ex. 175

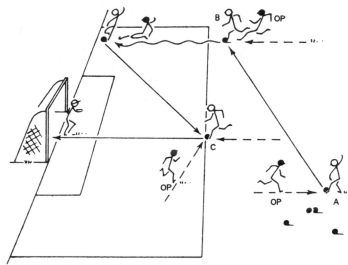

175

Participants   3 FP   3 OP   1 GK

Equipment   1 ball

Description   Player A stands with the ball in an inside left position. About 10 m in front of him is an OP. Player B stands inside right at the same level with an OP near him. Player C stands between A and B. His OP has taken position inside the penalty area. Player B suddenly sprints and is followed by his OP. A makes a strong, low pass into B's running path. B carries the ball forward quickly and dribbles it to the baseline avoiding interception by the OP. With the right timing, C runs into the open and receives a strong back pass from B. Before the OP can attack, C shoots at the goal.

Objectives   1. Strong low passing into a teammate's running path.
2. Carrying the ball along quickly.
3. Dribbling the ball quickly under opposing pressure.
4. Running into the open at the right moment.
5. Making a strong back pass into a teammate's running path.
6. Making a goal shot while running full speed.
7. Following up the goal shot.

Comments   Player C sprints to retrieve the ball shot at the goal and passes to A. All players quickly return to their starting positions. The OP do not attack seriously. The defense. however. may be geared to competition as time goes by.

Ex. 176

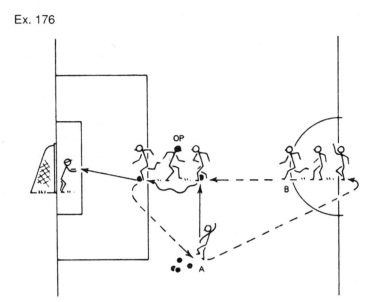

176

Participants   A = 2 FP   B = 2 - 4 FP   1 OP   1 GK

Equipment   1 ball for every player

Description   The players of group A stand, each with his ball level with the
             sideline of the penalty area, about 25 m from the baseline. The
             players of group B are in the central circle and the OP is on the
             penalty area boundary in front of the goal.
             The first player of group B sprints forward. A makes a strong, low
             pass into his running path. The OP immediately leaves the penalty
             area and runs toward B. Player B carries the ball forward quickly,
             outruns the OP with a body feint, and shoots at the goal from the
             penalty area boundary.

Objectives   1. Accurate, low, strong passing into a teammate's running path.
             2. Carrying the ball forward quickly.
             3. Dribbling the ball quickly with body feinting.
             4. Goal shot while running full speed after dribbling.
             5. Following up the goal shot.

Comments   The player who shoots at the goal sprints to retrieve the ball and
             goes quickly to the end of group A. The player who has passed runs
             to group B. The OP goes to his starting position each time. With less
             experienced players, a player of group A remains passer for a
             longer time. The positions are changed after a number of passes.

Ex. 177

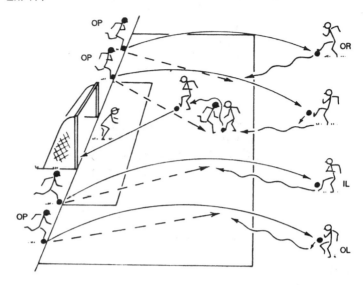

177

Participants   4 FO   4 FB or HB   1 GK

Equipment   1 ball for every player

Description: The FB stand, each with his ball, on the baseline, left and right of the goal. The FO are about 35 m from the baseline in their positions. The FB pass the resting balls high to the FO and immediately run toward them. Each FB tackles the FO to whom he passed the ball. The FO must dribble around his FB before he may shoot at the goal.

Objectives   1. Accurate, wide passing to a player.
2. Carrying the ball along quickly.
3. Correct dribbling.
4. Making an immediate goal shot after dribbling.
5. Following up the goal shot.

Comments   To avoid confusion, the FB should pass only when instructed by the CO. Only after the exercise is running smoothly can the FB all pass at the same time. The partners are chosen before hand by the CO. It may be necessary for the GK to react to many goal shots simultaneously.

Notes

Notes

Notes